Preface

These are trying times for amateur naturalists. In most parts of the civilized world, it is no longer possible to mount even modest collecting all manner of wildlife offered on dealers' lists, from exotic giant anteaters to Indigo Snakes. By the 1990s, the variety of animals available had

Green Iguana, *Iguana iguana*. Hardy and inexpensive, Green Iguanas, particularly small ones, make excellent aquaterrarium pets. Photo by Isabelle Francais.

expeditions for specimens. In the United States, where children have collected tadpoles and starfishes almost as a ritual part of growing up and exploring, such activities are now strictly regulated, often prohibited by laws or regulations. The political world is making attempts to enforce conservation, and in most cases these efforts are to be praised.

But these regulations have reduced the once copious flow of wildlife into the hands of both amateur and professional animal keepers. In the 1960s, it was not uncommon to see dropped sharply, and prices for those species on the market often rose dramatically. My first purchases of an iguana, tegu, Boa Constrictor and a Green Anole were very affordable, none costing more than a bag or two of groceries. Of course, this was back in the 1960's, and today some of these same animals can cost as much as an entire fishtank setup, equipment and all!

I present these facts to help clarify my position on amateur herpetoculture and aquaculture. Be assured, I am convinced of the positive roles played by

the amateur naturalists or I would not have written this book, or its earlier companion, **Giant Lizards**. I am not alone in this assessment. During the 1989 First World Congress of Herpetology, held in England, many professional herpetologists lamented the difficulty they had in studying their chosen animals. They extended these feelings to a concern about the effect such limitations may have on amateurs who may be enticed into biological careers (or just responsible, environmentally aware lives) if they, like most of us at the Congress, began our interests with captive herpetofauna. As a result of several symposia and informal meetings, a committee was formed to study and document the contributions to herpetology made by amateurs. I serve as co-chairman of the eight-member group, representing herpetologists from the United States, Germany, Australia, England, and France. Our initial position statement

on the validity of amateur herpetoculturists was endorsed by over 70 delegates from no less than 40 nations; almost all were professional herpetologists.

Also be assured that there are "bad apples" in the herpetocultural world who, through inhumane or irresponsible acts, bring hostility and fear from the lay public to our interests. With that in mind, here are my positions on amateur zookeeping:

First, though prices have indeed risen sharply in the past 20 years, the new prices are not all uncharacteristically high. In many cases, the current prices are high enough to discourage impulse buyers, and this has been at least part of the reason why herpetofauna and many other "pets" are no longer sold in chain department stores. It has been my experience that people tend to give more care and attention to something they have to pay more than pocket change to obtain. Probably the majority of available herpetofauna have become expensive

Boa Constrictor, *Boa constrictor*. The aquaterrarium that holds a Boa Constrictor should have plenty of sturdy branches for the animal to climb on. Photo by W. Wuster.

enough to limit their sale to casual buyers. Some animals are still reasonably priced so that novices and collectors with limited assets can still keep them. Tegus are one example, as are many anoles, frogs, one of that, a large number concentrated on a few species and learned to breed them reliably and repeatedly. Today, virtually no aquarium standard need be taken from the wild, for from guppies to

Dumeril's Monitor, *Varanus dumerili*. Most monitors do well in aquaterrarium setups, but housing the larger specimens might be very costly. Photo by R. T. Zappalorti.

invertebrates, and most tropical fishes. These last deserve a special consideration, for it is worthwhile to ask WHY fishes remain affordable while many other animals become prohibitively expensive, or disappear from the market.

Tropical fish hobbyists have long funnelled their efforts into breeding their charges. While many, perhaps most, aquarists kept community tanks and 'postage stamp collections' made up of one of this, and Neon Tetras to discus, they are largely bred by commercial and amateur breeders.

Reptile and amphibian people, however, lag far behind. 'Postage stamp' collections were traditionally the way for collectors to proceed. One eastern zoo even proclaimed, proudly, that it had one specimen of almost every known species and subspecies of rattlesnake. Leadership to breed animals was feeble, at best. As a consequence, when wildlife regulations and laws, such as the Lacey Act and the Convention on the International Trade in Endangered Species, were enforced, many herpetoculturists found their sources of specimens

severely limited, and many animals suddenly became extremely costly. The realities of this supply and demand scenario are still with us today, as demonstrated by the virtual doubling of the price for Dumeril's Monitors and then increased even farther when Thailand halted export of the species in 1988.

It should be obvious by now that 1) a variety of animals is still available, 2) supply of these animals is becoming limited, through depletion of natural populations and restrictions on exports, 3) many people are attempting to further limit WHO may own animals that are available, through restrictive and often ill-concieved regulations and laws, 4) prices will increase in response to these pressures and consumer demands, and 5) the responsible tact to take would seem to be that of enhancing captive breeding programs. Australian wildlife has been effectively barred from export for some two decades, yet bird breeders who owned zebra finches before the ban learned how to breed them. Today, you may purchase Zebra Finches at many pet shops for only a few dollars; had they not been bred in captivity before the ban, they may well command a several-hundred dollar price tag today, as do most Australian reptiles.

Then there is Madagascar, an island nation off Africa's southeastern coast, that had long prohibited the collection and export of its fauna. Over the past decade, Malagasy lumber has become a major source of income for this poor nation, and its forests have been levelled at a rate almost unparalleled in the

Madagascan Silver-eyed Treefrog, *Boophis rappoides*. Most of the Madagascan treefrogs make good captives, but they require very small food items, which may be difficult for some keepers to acquire. Photo by Paul Freed.

world. Along with this destruction, Malagasy herpetofauna has become another "cash crop," and species almost unknown in 1988 are now fairly familiar to herpetoculturists. Many of these animals, notably the day geckos and mantella frogs, are being bred with considerable success, and there is probably enough breeding stock now available that no new specimens would need to be removed from the wild. (Of course, Madagascar may have NO wild soon. Habitat destruction has no close competitor as the primary factor behind biotic extinctions). Along with this new access to Malagasy herpetofauna, the discovery and descriptions of many new species has resulted. It is truly awesome to contemplate that these animals, some quite beautiful in color and structure, could have been exterminated without ever being discovered by science had Madagascar protected animals while simultaneously destroying forests. Many rare species are already being kept successfully in captive collections.

There is hope. Herpetoculturists are breeding animals in record numbers, and their efforts are expanding, it seems, almost exponentially. The list of species that can be obtained, with considerable reliability, from captive bred sources includes: Boa Constrictors, rainbow boas,

anoles, Leopard Geckos, many day geckos, kingsnakes of many types, Corn Snakes, treefrogs, poison frogs, and even such Australian species as bearded dragons, blue-tongue skinks, and Carpet Pythons.

Anoles, *Anolis* sp., mating. Once an animal feels comfortable enough in its setup, it will begin to behave almost exactly as it would in the wild. Photo by the author.

I do not believe that just anybody with a few dollars should run out to purchase a pet, of ANY type. If dealers can make a few dollars to pay their expenses and earn a fair profit, fine. Consumers should carefully weigh the requirements of a potential animal purchase, and if the price tag is what slows them down to consider the impending responsibility, fine. The caring for ANY life is a responsibility, and when you presume to provide a home for a creature, you assume the role of a god to that creature: YOU must provide food, shelter, heat, water and safety. YOU must insure that it is compatible with other cage occupants, and that cage space is not unduly confining. Should the animals become ill, you must attempt to effect a cure.

Educated viviculturists (those who keep any small animals in their homes) are an asset. They often provide data not otherwise available to scientists about the habits of these wonderful animals. Through careful and selective breeding, animals will continue to be available to amateurs. These animals teach children about responsibility and caring for other living things. I have often used reptiles and fishes in classrooms to encourage my students to seek the wonders of nature, and with a high percentage of success. An esthetically pleasing home vivarium, especially one with the broad appeal of an aquaterrarium, helps keep nature alive and well in the minds of people who must confront the daily grind of urban work and suburban living. These people, acutely aware of the bounty within a jungle, are the ones who are almost guaranteed to support and promote conservation

Golden Mantella, *Mantella aurantiaca*. Mantella frogs are among the best aquaterrarium subjects, but they probably won't spend a great deal of time in the water. Photo by Robert S. Simmons.

efforts that we all need if we are to survive as a species. They know better than most the tragedy we face if our natural habitats are lost as the last tree is felled. Their attention is not limited to the one-hour television documentary. When the television show is over, they still share a piece of their living rooms with the rainforests and their amazing creatures.

A book like this is written as a labor of love. The subject is largely about esthetics, and supplements other, excellent texts on husbandry of aquaterrarium inhabitants. The knowledge of herpetoculture I have gained over these past three decades is a gift from many sources, some of whom I particularly thank here and now.

Aquaterrariums was inspired by the excellent German *Handbuch der Terrarienkunde* by Paul Heinrich Stettler, and *Das Paludarium*, by Ralf Blauscheck. There has not been, to my knowledge, an English-language book as holistic in its approach to the animals, plants, and decorum of vivariums as these magnificent works. The thorough illustrations make both books highly recommended even if you do not read a word of German (and should serve as inspiration to high school-aged naturalists to choose German as their foreign language). My gratitude to these authors for their examples.

Thanks also to my good friend Wolgang Bohme, of the Museum Alexander Koenig, Bonn, Germany, who for 20 years has supplied me with excellent German publications. I am also grateful to him for providing access to the live herpetofaunal exhibits at the Museum. Hans-Georg Horn similarly deluged me with valuable and greatly appreciated literature, as did the late H.G. Petzold of the Berlin Zoo.

Special thanks are in order for my long-time friend Gerry Swan, who often provded needed encouragement, and as frequently provided me with photographs and books from "downunda." Joseph T. Collins was my mentor for many years while I was at the University of Kansas; he taught me much about writing and editing, and how to maintain my sanity, while also putting me in touch with many of the best zoo herpetologists in the world.

Richard Wallace provided me with a new appreciation for amphibians, especially salamanders, while serving as my doctoral advisor at the University of Idaho. Much of the amphibian section reflects, I trust, his enthusiastic interest in these animals. I am also deeply indebted to him for providing me with lab and office space, and for his constant stream of useful reprints, and especially for the wonderful field trips that allowed me to sample so much of the herpetofauna of the Pacific Northwest.

Others who have most graciously allowed me access to specimens in their care for photographic or data gathering purposes include: Harry Greene (University of California, Berkeley), Doug King and Ron Roper (Atlantis Pet Shop, Los Gatos, CA), Owen Maercks (East Bay Vivarium, Berkeley, CA), and Michael Beale, Chera Aleknar, and Ken Howell (Steinhart Aquarium). For information of various sorts I thank Kenneth McCloud, Kenneth White, Chris Banks, and Raymond Hoser.

Caring for animals in my own home has often required Herculean assistance from otherwise sane people, most notably from my parents during those long-gone years of the 1960s, and, since 1987, Sabrina Hanson. I reserve, as ever, my special thanks to my truly better half, Teri. She would read the manuscript and keep

The author holding a Water Monitor, *Varanus salvator.*

me from lapsing into either jargon or Victorian prose. Her enthusiasm for my work never wanes, and I remain thankful to have her as my prime supporter.

ROBERT GEORGE
SPRACKLAND
Cupertino, California

Chapter 1
Introduction

What is an aquaterrarium, and why would there be a need for a book about such a subject?

The etymology of *aquaterrarium* is simple, meaning *water and land*. In the broadest sense, any vivarium (a container for living things) that has both an aquatic and a terrestrial component is an aquaterrarium. In Europe, the term employed is *paludarium*. These vivariums are extremely popular in zoos, as they can make spectacular, large exhibits, but they are still something of a novelty in many homes. This book is meant as a guide to start you along in construction, population, and maintenance of an aquaterrarium.

The decision to build an aquaterrarium entails some special concerns, for unlike other terrariums the aquaterrarium is generally larger, partially filled with permanent water, and is consequently going to be difficult and laborious to move after it has been established. In many cases, choice of location is a permanent decision. In addition, you must consider the intent of the container: is it to provide a naturalistic setting for a species you expect to breed in the vivarium, or is it to be used as an exhibit piece, perhaps with a variety of species? If you are constructing an aquaterrarium for use in a school or other space for public exhibition, you must take into account ways to prevent disturbing occupants of the vivarium. If you will periodically need to remove animals for student examination, you must have a simple way of extricating specimens without also having to destroy cage decor to find the specimens. In short, you must begin by asking *for what purpose is this setup to be used?*

The following chapters will detail each of these concerns and suggest ways of dealing with a new aquaterrarium. As part of the preliminary research for such an undertaking, an educated herpetoculturist should be well read on the subjects he for which he or she intends to care. An extensive bibliography is included at the end of this book, but a brief review of valuable literature for the novice is presented here. Any of these works will

Dr. Axelrod's Atlas of Freshwater Aquarium Fishes, Mini-Edition (H-1090), is an excellent guide for anyone who appreciates the freshwater fishkeeping hobby. It contains almost a thousand pages of both reliable text and beautiful full-color photography.

PS-876, 384
pages, **over
175 color
photos**.

H-1077, over
1150 pages,
**over 7000
color photos**.

H-1102, 830
pages, over
**1800 color
photos**.

offer suggestions about terrariums or aquariums and the creatures to be kept in each medium, land and water.

Perhaps the most comprehensive book on tropical fishes is *Dr. Axelrod's Mini-Atlas of Tropical Freshwater Fishes*, published by T.F.H. If I were to recommend one book for the serious amateur, this would be my choice. Important features include detailed descriptions of aquarium fishes and plants and decoration, how to set up breeding facilities, and descriptions of plants.

Finally, *Dr. Axelrod's Atlas of Freshwater Aquarium Fishes* is a major picture book for the identification of literally thousands of aquarium species. It is also an esthetically pleasing book (as is the herptile *Atlas* described below) that would be welcomed by any serious hobbyist.

Books on herpetoculture include *The Completely Illustrated Atlas of Reptiles and Amphibians for the Terrarium* by Obst, Richter, and Jacob. Written by some of eastern Europe's most knowledgable herpetologists, this English (T.F.H.) translation includes information on an overwhelming array of animals, and details all

aspects of husbandry. If you are a novice and can purchase only one guide book, this is the best choice. If you have some terrarium experience, you will find many helpful ideas in *Reptiles and Amphibians, Care, Behavior, Reproduction* by Elke Zimmermann. Chapters on nutrition and the breeding of amphibians are especially informative, and even the novice herpetoculturist will benefit from Ms. Zimmermann's expertise.

Another general work is Chris Mattison's *The Care of Reptiles and Amphibians in Captivity*, a small but comprehensive volume covering general terrarium care, and specific information about many of the more commonly available species of herpetofauna.

One excellent English-language periodical that can be recommended is *Tropical Fish Hobbyist*, a monthly magazine that features informative updates on the aquarium hobby, including information on improving aquaculture techniques. In October, 1989 the magazine began covering herpetological subjects with an article on Chinese crocodile lizards and their care in aquaterrariums. This column is now a regular feature of the magazine.

There are, of course, numerous other publications, many of which are restricted to a group or even a single species. With experience, the novice will decide what areas to specialize in and pursue. Much information can be obtained from other hobbyists, and there are numerous regional aquarium and herpetological societies that provide newsletters and meetings so members may exchange information, literature, and specimens.

A typical aquaterrarium, designed with live plants and plastic boundaries. Photo by the author.

Chapter 2
Basics

The basics of vivarium culture include container dimensions, design and location, substrate, size of aquarium component, filtration of water and cleaning of land areas, and providing adequate and appropriate heat and light for the inhabitants. It is of primary importance to determine the purpose of the vivarium, as all decisions regarding outfitting the structure are linked to its function.

THE VIVARIUM
The container that will house your miniature environment is the vivarium, and you have two options for obtaining a suitable container: *buy one or build one.* Available for purchase are the glass and plexiglas aquariums that

range in size from very small to very large. There are distinct pros and cons to conventional aquariums. Among the positive features are 1) ready availability at pet stores, 2) they are built specifically to hold water, 3) aquarium accessories are built specifically for commercially available tanks.

The nature of an aquaterrarium makes it likely that some water will inevitably find its way to the "dry" land area of the enclosure. Because many plants and land animals will require a limited amount of soaking, the larger the container, the more likely it will be to work properly. Exceptions can be made for containers where the entire floor area will be aquatic, above which will be branches for small climbing creatures such as treefrogs. But many containers will require a dry land area, and this is very difficult to assure in a container of small dimensions, say

Right: Aqauterrariums don't need to be enormous—you can make a perfectly acceptable scaled-down setup for one or two small frogs or a single salamander. Photo courtesy of Hagen.
Below: Whatever size setup you desire, you'll certainly have no trouble getting an appropriate-size tank. Check your local pet shop to see what they have. Photo courtesy of Hagen.

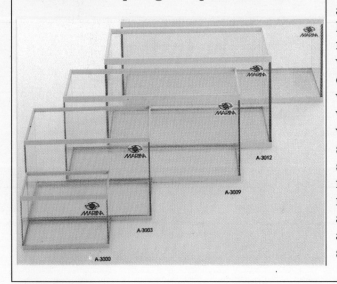

under 36 x 18 in/91.4 x 45.7cm.

There are two simple solutions to water containment in a commercially purchased aquarium. The first involves having a piece of glass or plexiglas cut to transect the container. The sides and bottom will be glued to the aquarium with an aquarium sealant. It is advisable to apply the

no problem exiting the pool if you use this design, but many turtles, small lizards, and amphibians will have trouble getting out of the water. A more useful design would be to install the divider at some sharp angle, providing a slope to make leaving the water far easier for the animals. Additionally, this divider may be enhanced by gluing rounded stones or gravel to

An otherwise lifeless setup can be spiced up by adding a piece of scenic sheeting to the back wall. Photo courtesy of Creative Surprizes.

sealant to both surfaces of this glass divider, that is, to the surface that will be immersed in water and the surface that will face the dry substrate. If this divider is positioned so that it is perpendicular to the floor of the container, you create a sharp drop from land to water. Larger lizards, snakes, and crocodilians should have

its surface, again with the aquarium sealant. This can provide both traction and decoration to the aquatic area. It is easier to glue these stones to the glass before gluing the glass into the aquaterrarium.

The other method for providing a water area is to place a smaller aquarium inside the larger one. Many low aquariums are now available, and these can be inserted directly into the large container. Of course, these containers will have vertical sides, and tend to be comparatively large, making their use only for large aquaterrariums the most advantageous.

Many possibilities exist for containers where the bottom is entirely made of an aquarium some several inches deep. These designs are useful and attractive when housing fishes, large aquatic amphibians, aquatic turtles, and many invertebrates. Above this aquarium can be placed a variety of branches and vines, in which live treefrogs, small geckos, and other species that are usually off the ground.

Alternatively, you can build, or arrange to have built, a custom aquaterrarium to your specifications. This alternative may or may not involve less expense than purchasing a standard aquarium, but it provides the advantage of having special design features constructed into the unit. For example, draining the water from a standard aquarium could be a complicated chore that involves greatly disturbing the residents of the container. But a custom aquarium unit, say with a drain built into its floor, can make this necessary operation a relatively simple procedure, causing the least stress and work for both the keeper and his charges. If you are working on your first aquaterrarium and have limited experience with either the aquatic or terrestrial animals you plan to keep, your simplest option would be the standard aquarium, perhaps in the 40 to 60 gallon range, and save the complexity of a custom container until you have experience in keeping such a vivarium.

In addition to considering physical dimensions of your intended paludarium, consideration must also be given to its location. Once filled with water, gravel, plants and animals, it will not be a simple matter to move the setup. It is always best to establish a vivarium

Southern Painted Turtle, *Chrysemys picta dorsalis*. Juvenile specimen. Painted Turtles seem to do remarkably well in aquaterrarium setups. Photo by W. P. Mara.

where you can control the overall environment within, which means that a good location will be away from drafts or uncovered windows that allow uncontrolled amounts of housekeeping concerns that enter into the choice of location for the aquaterrarium. If it is to be located in a central area of the home, say a living room, can cleanup chores,

Eastern Painted Turtle, *Chrysemys picta picta.* Juvenile specimen. As with so many other aquaterrarium animals, Painted Turtles are best acquired when they are small. Photo by W. P. Mara.

sunlight to enter. If a vivarium is to contain many tropical species, proximity to a window may be advantageous, especially if the window can be screened to shut out sunlight on particularly hot days. This same proximity to a window may mean that the area where the aquaterrarium is situated may become cool during winter months, making it difficult to keep internal temperatures high enough for the occupants.

There are also practical

such as water changes or soil removal, be accomplished without undue difficulty? What are the consequences of a water spill onto the carpet or nearby furniture? What could be damaged if an animal escapes? Could a family pet, such as a dog or cat, or a small child do damage to the terrarium, or cause a foreseeable accident to occur?

Terrarium animals frequently cause some odors (a sign that some water or soil change is

Make life easy on yourself—purchase a device that will help you clean your aqua-terrarium(s) so you end up doing as little work as possible. Such products can be found at many pet shops. Photo courtesy of Aquarium Products.

needed), so, unlike a strict aquarium, this type of vivarium is probably not suitable for an area where food is served, e.g., dining rooms. In many cases, the best solution is to have a specific room where the aquaterrarium can be kept with minimal inconvenience to other house residents and guests.

SUBSTRATES

The choice of substrate for an aquaterrarium is more a matter of esthetics than necessity. Consideration should also follow the route of least resistance in regards to keeping the vivarium clean and pleasant in appearance between cleanings.

The substrate for the aquarium portion of the paludarium can conceivably be bare, unadorned glass, especially in larger or custom-built containers that have an external filtration system. Most first or household aquaterrariums will probably not be either so large or complex that this option will be viable, and the keeper will elect to have an undergravel filter as the water-cleansing system of choice. Plastic undergravel filters require something heavy on top of them lest they float, and in most cases the best substrate is aquarium gravel. Pet shops now stock an incredible array of gravels, from tiny colored chips to smooth pea gravel to fairly large rocks, the latter two in natural hues. Colored gravels can be mixed to give an interesting and somewhat natural appearance that will enhance visibility of fishes and aquatic amphibians without making the organisms unduly conspicuous. Mixtures of green or blue and black present a pleasing background for light and highly reflective-colored fishes. Many aquarists have opted for the natural sand-hued gravels, and these certainly look fine in the aquaterrarium.

Gravel has the advantage of being easily cleaned by removal and rinsing. This process will be necessary from time to time, coincident with major water changes, to remove algae and odor-causing microorganisms. However, another good aquatic substrate includes a gravel-peat mixture. Such a combination is useful if a particularly natural environmental picture is the goal, and though it requires greater effort to keep clean (through more frequent water changes, a stronger and more reliable pump than a simple gravel substrate would need) it is easy to prepare and offers a change from the standard gravel-bottomed aquarium.

Several options are available for the land area of the container. Again, gravel can be used for many species of reptiles such as turtles, some snakes, larger lizards and crocodilians, but may be too abrasive for many soft skinned species, including most amphibians. Animals that need to burrow as part of the normal life cycle, such as many toads and ambystomatid salamanders (e.g., Tiger, Spotted and Jefferson's Salamanders being some of the species in question) will find gravel an unacceptable substrate. For these animals I

Pine Barrens Treefrog, *Hyla andersoni*. Treefrogs in general seem to respond well to life in an aquaterrarium. This particular species is heavily protected by environmental law. Photo by R. T. Zappalorti.

Tiger Salamander, *Ambystoma tigrinum.* Ambystomid salamanders are hardy and attractive, but most of them like to burrow and thus probably won't be seen all that often. Photo by the author.

Alpine Newt, *Triturus alpestris.* Newts are perhaps the salamanders best-suited for life in the aquaterrarium setup. Photo by the author.

recommend a substrate of potting soil, found in any garden store. The bottom of the land area should have a layer of large, smooth gravel as a base, to allow some drainage of the soil. Many herpetoculturists suggest using a liberal amount of aquarium filter charcoal in this base layer, which may help control odors. Above this, pack potting soil. To facilitate housekeeping, put a buffer area of gravel near the edge of the aquarium section, providing an area for small animals to "lose" some adhering soil before they enter the water. If larger species are kept, such as iguanas or monitors, there is very little that can successfully be done to keep water clean for long if soil is employed as a substrate.

For the larger species, gravel remains the simplest solution. Since the gravel must be at least as deep as the aquarium portion, you can see how the aquaterrarium can quickly become quite heavy even if the physical dimensions are modest. Remember that even large lizards tend to dig a great deal, especially if adequate shelter for complete concealment is absent. To keep the land gravel from migrating into the water, provide plenty of large boxes, bark, and branches for each resident.

If you are customizing an aquaterrarium, you may wish to build a platform that is level with the top of the sunken pool of water. A solid platform can then be left bare, covered with artificial turf, or have smooth gravel glued to its surface, depending on the type of animals you will house and the specificity of their environmental demands.

animals that are housed in aquaterrariums. They may poison water for fishes, be ingested and poison or choke amphibians and reptiles, and they are notorious for holding unpleasant odors. Shavings cannot be cleaned and reused, but must be completely replaced. In short, they offer no advantages and should be scrupulously avoided.

Vermiculite is also used by many terrarium

Kiamichi Slimy Salamander, *Plethodon kiamichi*. Most of the slimy salamanders do well in captivity, but they should not be handled due to the substances secreted from their skin. Photo by Suzanne L. and Joseph T. Collins.

A variety of wood bark chips, corncob, and shavings are used in terrariums, with mixed results. Corncob may be ingested by larger specimens and can cause gut obstructions leading to death. Wood chips often contain dust and small insects, so they must be thoroughly washed and dried before being used in the terrarium. Wood shavings, usually sold as cedar, redwood, or pine, are generally dangerous to the

keepers, most typically for small, sand-dwelling reptiles and as a medium to hold incubating reptile eggs. As a substrate in an aquaterrarium it is limited in usefulness. It offers little traction for larger (over 8 in/20.3 cm) animals, is dispersed more readily than potting soil (being almost impossible to keep out of the water), and retains moisture, including animal wastes, more readily than better substrates.

FILTRATION AND CLEANING

Filtration of the paludarium's water will be new for some herpetoculturists; it is old hat for aquarists. This discussion presumes that some wholly aquatic organisms, such as fishes and crustaceans, will be resident in the aquaterrarium, and that the responsibility for the aquaterrarist is more complex than simply offering ordinary tap water to the environment.

The water of this environment will contain bacteria and chemicals that will affect the lives of resident animals and plants in both positive and negative ways. The osmotic pressure of freshwater

animals is such that water tends to transport into the body rapidly. To keep from literally bursting, these organisms excrete excess water, and many waste products, constantly. This means that the organisms are constantly dumping quantities of ammonia, nitrates, nitrites, and food excreta into the water. If these toxins accumulate, the water can no longer support the organisms and they will die. It is the function of filtration to remove these toxins from the water. In addition, a good filter will remove large, particles from the water, particles that cause water to become cloudy and inhibit viewing of the organisms in the aquarium.

The simplest filtration system for a relatively shallow aquarium such as that in the aquaterrarium is the undergravel filter. This is a rectangular plastic plate with numerous slits along the upper surface. It sits on the bottom of the aquarium, and is covered by the substrate, usually gravel. Air is pumped under the filter, lowering pressure beneath the gravel. As a result, water "falls" down through the gravel as air bubbles rise out the airstem, making a vacuum cleaner that is always in operation. Because the debris sucked down through the gravel is denser than the air rising up the airstem, the debris is trapped under the gravel, where microorganisms consume many of the toxins, leaving a harmless residue behind.

Undergravel filters are extremely simple to set up and operate, for they have no components such as coal or floss to change and the only mechanical part is the air pump. Some filter cartridges are available and recommended. On occasion it will be necessary to clean the accumulated material from under the filter. The time interval for this task depends upon the number of resident animals, the amount of soil getting into the water, and the rate at which water becomes unpleasant to view. You know it is time for a complete cleaning when 1) water is brown and opaque, 2) the aquaterrarium has an unpleasant smell, and 3) the aquatic substrate is visibly dirty.

Aquarists have long had benefit of an underwater vacuum cleaner, called a *siphon*, which allows you to remove debris from gravel and coarse sand without having to physically remove the substrate from the tank. In the same way that a siphon (available from virtually every pet shop)

cleans gravel, it can be inserted all the way down through the substrate to the top of the undergravel filter and can vacuum the material out from under the filter. Because the material under the filter contains many useful bacteria, be sure not to remove all the debris. In fact, a complete water-substrate change, coupled with cleaning out everything under the filter, may result in the deaths of many fishes because a finely-tuned microhabitat has been so drastically altered.

The function of an undergravel filter is dependent upon the flow of air up the airstem. This is usually situated in a back corner of the aquarium. The water level in an

Left: There are a number of tonic-like formulas manufactured to treat not only the animals that live in an aquarium or aquaterrarium, but also the water itself. Photo courtesy Hagen.

Undergravel filters work well with aqua-terrariums. These are offered in a variety of sizes and can be properly maintained with a minimum of effort on the keeper's part. Photo courtesy of Hagen.

Most aqua-terrariums can make use of an undergravel filter. Most of them are reasonably priced and can be found at your local pet shop. Photo courtesy of Hagen.

aquaterrarium may be quite lower than is customary in traditional aquariums, so the airstem will typically have to be sawed to a shorter height. The upper level of the pipe should be about 0.5 in/ 1.25 cm beneath the water level. If the top of the pipe is above water level, the filter cannot work.

As convenient as an undergravel filter may be for small aquariums, it is limited in usefulness in larger tanks, or those containing animals particularly noted for dirtying the water. For most aquarium fishes, crayfishes, freshwater crabs, frogs, and newts, the undergravel filter will

suffice even for a large aquarium. Animals, such as large fishes (and goldfishes), aquatic turtles, crocodilians, large snakes, and lizards, tend to leave residue in the water that cannot be filtered by an undergravel unit. For this type of aquaterrarium, an undergravel filter should be supplemented with a conventional outside filter. In essence, an outside filter is a box kept outside of the vivarium, often hanging from the back of the container. The filter contains materials, such as spun glass, crushed charcoal, or diatoms, which act something like a sieve to remove large particles from the water. Because filter materials accumulate waste products from aquarium water, they must be changed frequently, perhaps weekly for a large aquarium, or one with particularly soil-producing organisms. Many filters are equipped with inserts that contain charcoal and floss,

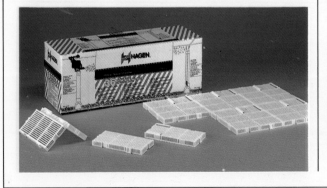

small to provide a large enough surface area for sufficient oxygen to enter water. Fishes and amphibians extract oxygen through gills and the skin at a rate often exceeding the capacity of the tank to exchange fresh oxygen from the air. Bubblers, including airstones and filters, greatly increase oxygen replenishment to the aquarium water.

and these can usually be removed, washed with fresh water (NEVER with soap!), and reused once or twice.

Both undergravel and outside filters also aerate water by bubbling air into the aquarium. The undergravel filter pumps air down a hose under the filter, which is then bubbled at the top of the airstem, while the outside filter splashes water back into the aquarium, thus adding trapped air to the return water flow. Bubbling in an aquarium is not only a pleasant sight, it is essential for many organisms. The basic aquarium is simply too

Cleaning the aquarium portion of a paludarium is not overly complicated. Siphons make cleaning of the gravel a simple process

There are a great many filter pumps to be considered; make sure you are getting the right one for your tank and filter. photo courtesy of Hagen.

Tank cleaning is the most effective preventive medicine practice you can perform. There are a great number of products designed to make this task as easy as possible; they are a worthy investment. Check with your local pet dealer to find what products they offer. Photo courtesy of Hagen.

that does not require removal of occupants. It will rarely be necessary to conduct a complete water change if a proper filtration system is installed (except, in most cases, for some aquatic turtles and most crocodilians), but when necessary to do this, removal of animals is important. A standard siphon hose can be used to empty an aquarium, or, if you can customize a container, equip it with a bottom drain. With the latter, once all the water is drained, substrate can be cleaned by rinsing and then allowing the dirty water to drain out the bottom of the tank. If you use a siphon, substrate may have to be removed and rinsed. In some cases, complete replacement of the substrate may be the best option for cleanliness. Whenever possible during substrate cleaning, I suggest allowing cleaned substrate to dry naturally in sunlight. There are labor-saving water changes available at most pet shops.

New water can be put into the aquarium while gravel is outside being cleaned and dried. Be sure to add whatever chemicals are needed to neutralize chlorine and chloramines that may be present in your tap water. Since the chemical additives of tap water vary from community to community, check with your local pet shop aquarist to find out what will be needed for treating your particular water supply.

HEAT AND LIGHT

Heating aquariums is an easy procedure, for completely submersible, thermostatically controlled heaters are available in a variety of sizes, shapes, and wattages. In many aquaterrariums, the heater will be positioned against the glass at the rear of the aquarium section (where it can be easily concealed from view) in a horizontal, rather than the more typical vertical, position. Set the thermostat at an appropriate temperature,

plug in the unit, and you are done. **Be sure to use a submersible, waterproof heater!**

Tropical organisms will need warm water in the range of 70 to 78°F/21 to 25°C, and these usually require a heater, especially during the winter if you live in a temperate zone. Many organisms, however, will not need a heater to survive, and these include goldfishes, guppies, some mollies, and most amphibians.

Heat for the terrestrial portion of a paludarium is a bit more involved. Uniform heat distribution is not generally recommended because poikilothermic animals control their temperatures by thermal shuttling—the movement from warm

A lighted aquarium hood with a flip-top lid will make feedings easy, and cast an attractive light into the enclosure. Photo courtesy of Hagen.

Correct lighting is essential for all captive animals, and, in some cases, the correct *type* of light (usually referred to as *full-spectrum* lighting), must also be considered. Photo courtesy of Energy Savers.

to cool places during the day, allowing a near-constant body temperature within specific, preferred limits. A uniformly heated terrarium may leave no room for a cool respite from heat, excepting the water, and many organisms will not readily enter the water to cool down. The optimal situation, then, is to provide a thermal gradient.

The concept behind a thermal gradient is that you provide an area of warmth in excess of what is needed, and enough space in the vivarium so that as you move from the hottest spot, the temperatures become lower. In a paludarium, the warmest spot should be either the land furthest from the water section, or near the top of the terrarium. Animals can reach the

latter by climbing whatever props (e.g., logs, large plants) you include in the container. Because the aquaterrarium is a simulation of a forested area, keeping the hottest area near the top of the container is preferable to heating the soil. Animals in

this environment are adapted to climb in search of heat, and the cooler soil is a source of refuge for many animals. Thus, the recommendation is that you equip a corner of the enclosure with a heat lamp, and use smaller incandescent or fluorescent bulbs to provide light for the rest of the container. Heat tapes, used outside and under the terrarium in many cases, are not especially recommended for the aquaterrarium, because they produce heat from the wrong orientation—beneath the animals. Electrically heated "hot rocks" also produce heat from below and animals rest on them until they are warm.

Heat rises, as all elementary physics students will tell you. Consequently, the heat lamp will need to be strong enough to deliver a region of warmth to a spot down

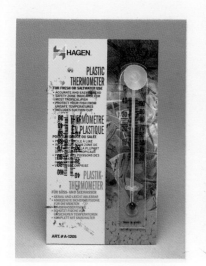

into the terrarium. This is rarely a problem, but can be facilitated by the simple addition of a fan near the lamp. The fan will both move warm air down into the terrarium and also provide air circulation in the container. Few forests are devoid of a breeze, but a glass and wood aquaterrarium will certainly lack such air movement unless it is supplied artificially. Small fans are now available at low prices, including battery operated units used in cars that are sold in many gas stations and convenience stores. The fan should blow air down from near the heat lamp, which will allow air to circulate down, across the land and water areas, then rise over the water. This will also help keep humidity from becoming oppressive in the aquaterrarium, and help

Do yourself, and your animals, a favor, and purchase a reliable thermometer so you will always be able to accurately monitor the temperature inside your aquaterrarium setup. Photo courtesy Hagen.

It is advised that you purchase two separate thermometers for your aqua-terrarium—one for the air temperature and the other for the water. A tank that is too hot or too cold will endanger the lives of its inmates. Photo courtesy Hagen.

A pair of Alpine Newts, *Triturus alpestris*. Note the dorsal crest on the male below. Photo by L. Wischnath.

keep glass over the water from misting up, obscuring viewing.

What is "hot enough" for terrestrial animals in a tropical vivarium? The area nearest the heat lamp should be around 82 to 90°F/28 to 32°C for a large (over 30 x 18 x 24 in/76.2 x 45.7 x 60.9 cm) aquaterrarium, 80 to 84°F/ 26 to 29°C for a smaller container. The important factor is to be sure that the coolest area is cool enough to provide a safe refuge from the heat. At night, when the lights are out, the temperature may drop considerably—to about 62°F/17°C. as it does in many tropical localities.

Chapter 3
Decorating

An enterprise as complex as an aquaterrarium is first and foremost an exhibition, i.e., a centerpiece to a room in the home of a naturalist. It may be intended as a microhabitat for breeding some species, but this is often better accomplished in far simpler, more modest facilities. With its combination of land and water, an assortment of exotic plants and selected animals, an aquaterrarium is just too extraordinary a creation to be anything as "merely" functional as another terrarium.

Consequently, many people will construct an aquaterrarium because of the decorating possibilities it will offer. The herpetoculturist is now able to express some artistic skills. The new challenge is to capture, in as realistic a way as possible, the microhabitat of a piece of tropical forest adjacent to a pond or stream. It is an esthetic challenge, unlike that usually offered in establishing most conventional terrariums, and greatly expanding the possibilities aquarists have long been able to pursue.

It is my assumption in this book that your plan to build an aquaterrarium is based on desire to have a small sample of a realistic setting in your home. I shall therefore not include discussions on the use of fluorescent-colored gravels, plastic plants, toy submarines, dinosaurs, and other common, but decidedly unnatural, aquarium accessories.

Scenic sheeting is offered in a variety of tableaux and can be found for sale in many pet shops. Photo courtesy Creative Surprizes.

In an aquaterrarium with a completely aquatic base (e.g., no land area) the bulk of the non-aquatic area will need to be an arboreal microhabitat. This means an environment made of branches, plastic or live plants such as vines, and other above-water props. In many cases, dead tree limbs will suffice as the main upright materials, and these are readily available in many places. Of course, natural materials brought in from outside often and typically contain numerous undesirable organisms, including mites, ticks, and potentially pathogenic bacteria. To be safe, such woody materials should be washed in water and allowed to dry, preferably in an oven, so as to kill any particularly hardy microorganisms.

Commercially available bark is a good material to form a backdrop with. It is lightweight, easy to apply, and can be used to provide support for vines and other long-stemmed plants. In addition, bark provides good traction for most climbing animals, which will probably make up the bulk of an aquaterrarium's terrestrial species. Bark can additionally be used to supplement the cage accessories, for being light in weight it will make excellent cover material. A small lizard or frog can hide under bark with little fear of the animal being crushed; such is not always true of rock, and

Above:
Artificial plants can be washed and used over again, and do not need maintenance. Photos courtesy of Hagen.

many a valuable animal has shifted the substrate enough to allow the covering rock to crush and kill the specimen.

A possible drawback to bark is that small flakes may come loose and get into the water. In fact, if large lizards are housed in the enclosure, such incidents will be quite routine. However good of a filtration system you employ, much of this woody debris will float, and need to be removed with a fine mesh net, in the same manner that one would skim a swimming pool.

Design of the aquaterrarium should definitely include a major allocation of space for vertical props, for most terrestrial species in such

an environment tend to be arboreal. In fact, barring turtles and crocodilians, most herpetofauna that is to be housed in such a container is very likely to be aloft, and may rarely come to the ground at all. The advantage of a vertical arrangement is that it gives you fully three dimensions to work with, and, provided enough perching sites can be offered, allows an unusual opportunity for species diversity that would be impossible in a standard terrarium of similar length and width. Unless you plan to house only one or two large animals in a large vivarium, provide as many

Above: Most scenic sheets come in two general types—those designed for herptiles, and those for fishes. Be sure to get the right one for the animals you have. Photo courtesy of Hagen.

Left: Most salamanders make good aquaterrarium subjects, but many of them, like this beautiful Ringed Salamander, *Ambystoma annulatum*, are highly secretive and thus will need a great deal of cover. Photo by K.T. Nemuras.

An aqua-terrarium, with heavy emphasis on moss-covered logs as the land body. Such a setup would be useful for many salamander and frog species. Photo by the author.

horizontal and angled branches as possible into your cage.

The centerpiece of the aquaterrarium's decor will usually be the plants you choose to include. If you are housing large, active lizards, such as monitors or adult iguanas, then you had best dispense of any plans to have an elaborately planted terrarium. These species are frequently to be seen digging through soil, uprooting most plants the same day that the animals are placed in the container. These lizards, by virtue of their bulk, may also simply wander over the plants, killing them as they are crushed. Unless you are converting a zoo exhibit or an entire room into a vivarium, save potted plants for cages with smaller animals.

Having said that, the variety of options for terrarium planting are virtually unlimited. There are three major factors to consider in planting your terrarium: Are the plants suited to the microhabitat? Are the plants safe for the animal residents? Can you provide proper care for the plants?

Are plants suited to the microhabitat of your aquaterrarium? If your substrate is to be kept dry, then you need plants that can tolerate dry soil conditions. I recommend that plants for the terrarium be planted in their pots, the pots buried beneath the surface level. However, soil moisture can still enter the soil in the pot, or seep from the pot into the soil. Similarly, plants requiring moist soil would not be suited for a terrarium using dry wood chips as a substrate. Many low vines will thrive and grow rapidly in a vivarium that allows them to remain moist constantly. Other plants, such as orchids and African violets, will do poorly in such conditions. Orchids require moisture, but only in well-drained soil, while African violets thrive in drier soil, with rare watering. Fortunately, most garden shops have knowledgeable staffs, and most plants come marked with care instructions, so choosing appropriate greenery is not a problem.

Are the plants you have chosen safe for the animal residents? Tropical frogs and salamanders are unlikely to encounter many cacti in their natural habitats. If they leap from a perch to the ground (a common way to transport themselves) such animals may easily be injured or killed if they should land upon, and be impaled by, a cactus. I have known people who have had this happen to their animals. Equally problematical is the question of plant toxicity to animals. Some plants may contain toxins that move cross-surface membranes (e.g., skin) and can harm herptiles. These plants include poison ivy and poison oak. Then there are plants that contain toxins that must be ingested to become dangerous, and include hemlock, milkweed, and many other plants.

Green Iguana, *Iguana iguana.* Large Green Iguanas are best kept outdoors, perhaps in a penned-in aquaterrarium setup. Such a setup, arranged properly, would take a great amount of time and effort, but would be very impressive. Photo by Robert S. Simmons.

An attractive domestic aquaterrarium with low emphasis on the water body. Note the *Shinisaur* sp. moving about the enclosure. Such a setup would be functional for many lizard species. Photo by the author.

Biologists have long considered the relationships between plants and insects as a biological arms race, the plants developing better, more intricate poisons as insects evolve better immunity. Vertebrates are not as actively involved in this arms race as are insects, and so many plants are potentially lethally toxic to terrarium animals. Some of the more commonly available poisonous plants include:

Bluebonnets
Bottlebrush
Buttercups
Christmas Rose
Crocus
Dogwood (fruit)
Ivy
Euphorbia
Four O'Clock
Lily of the valley
Morning Glory
Peony
Poppy (except California poppy)
Redwood (chips are highly toxic)
Tiger Lily

In many cases, indigestible plants can be safely kept with organisms that will not eat them, for the plant must be ingested to become dangerous. This

requires an adequate knowledge of the animals you are housing. Many familiar species are well-studied and can be assumed to abstain from herbivory. Others, though, are not so well known, and may surprise a keeper when they begin to forage on the foliage.

Can you provide adequate care for the plants you will house? Plants are not animals, but they often require care equal to or in excess of that necessary for the animals in your care. The diversity of plant life is extensive. Orchids alone currently count for some 26,000 species, equal to the total number of described fishes, or about the same as all the known amphibians, reptiles, birds, and mammals combined. Plants of this sort will have a wide variety of care requirements, for example, many need roots that are exposed to air or are kept in very well-drained substrate, and most require monthly doses of plant food. The point to remember is that plants typically require more than a little water from time to time. This primer is not the

An aqua-terrarium setup where the land and water masses were delineated by the inclusion of a plastic pane attached via silicone sealant. Such a feature can be added with little effort, but doing it neatly can be quite difficult. Photo by the author.

Spiny-tail Monitor, *Varanus acanthurus.* Most varanids can be kept in aquaterrarium setups, with equal emphasis on the land and water bodies. Photo by K. H. Switak.

place to obtain detailed information on plant care, for the subject is far too broad. A source of information for the novice would be the library on plants published by *Sunset Publications*, available at most nurseries and garden centers of department stores. *Sunset* is essentially the equivalent to *Tropical Fish Hobbyist Publications*, the former producing plant care volumes, the latter pet care books.

Aquatic plants will enhance the aquarium section of the aquaterrarium, and a wide variety of species is available from most better pet shops. Again, it is better to avoid using such live plants if large animals, that will continually disturb the water, are the creatures you choose to keep. If small turtles are in the aquaterrarium, they may feed upon some of these plants, making it necessary to replace them frequently. If aquatic plants die, they decompose quickly, and will dirty the water if not removed promptly. Most are fairly hardy, in an environment with a sizeable aquarium, and along with terrestrial inhabitants that include amphibians, small lizards, or small snakes, they make an esthetically pleasing addition to the flora and decor of the paludarium environment.

This brings us to consideration of the overall design of the paludarium: *Is it merely to be an extravagant exhibition piece, or will it simulate an actual geographic microcosm?* Perhaps I am biased by having been both a teacher and museum resident for so much of my life, but I opt for the ecologically accurate model, with its educational value intact. Consider the difference between a vivarium with Amazon swordplants (Brazil), Red-tailed Black Sharks (Thailand), and Wall Lizards (England), and one with Amazon swordplants, neon tetras,

To further your knowledge on the subject of plants that would be suitable for aquaterrarium usage, TFH has two excellent volumes on the subject— *Aquarium Plants* (H-966), and *A Complete Introduction to Aquarium Plants* (CO-002S). Check your pet shop for these titles.

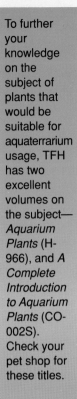

Smooth Newt, *Triturus vulgaris*. Newts can be fed a variety of small food items, most of which are readily available at pet shops. Photo by L. Wischnath.

If you have the space, you can consider setting up a fairly good-sized aquaterrarium for large aquatic turtles like the three Red-eared Slider, *Trachemys scripta elegans*, shown here. Photo by the author.

Facing page: A setup with low emphasis on water is perfectly adequate for reptiles that are only mildly aquatic, like the Crocodile Lizards, *Shinisaurus crocodilurus*, that seem to be enjoying themselves here. Photo by the author.

iguanas, and anoles, all South American. Granted that the animals and plants probably do not recognize each other to any significant extent, but if we, as herpetoculturists, are claiming an interest in preserving wildlife, should we not also preserve a piece of the actual microcosm as closely as possible?

Such an undertaking is really not much extra work. Herpetoculturists and aquarists are usually well aware of where their animals come from in nature, and most plants are labelled with both care instructions and origin. In either case, there are

plenty of books that can provide additional information, as can many shop keepers. Other excellent sources of information can come from visits to museums, zoos, and botanical gardens, all of which will be both highly informative and entertaining. Part of the joy in aquaterrarium construction is the research that precedes the finished product. When the whole assemblage is ready for display, it will reflect your time, effort, and research. It can be quite a rewarding challenge, and is the stuff of exhibition designers at the best zoos and museums.

Conehead Lizard, *Laemanctus serratus*. Most lizard species will appreciate plants and branches on which to climb and hide in. Photo by the author.

If you have the luxury of a great amount of water space in your aquaterrarium, you may want to consider giving it over to some good-sized fish.

Chapter 4
Residents

There is almost no limit to the types of animals that can be housed in an aquaterrarium, from insects and nematodes to small birds and mammals. However, many of these organisms fall into the categories of overly exotic, rarely kept, or have very special needs. Because the intent of this book is to serve as a primer, it is inappropriate to include coverage of unduly exotic, large, or demanding organisms. For that reason, I shall confine my comments to include hardy organisms from the subphylum Crustacea, and the vertebrate classes Osteichthyes, Amphibia, and Reptilia*. Even so, this includes a vast assembly of organisms, and my discussion will be limited to general concepts applicable for easily curated animals.

---

*The terms *class* and *Reptilia* are used in the historical sense, e.g., *Reptilia* is composed of turtles, crocodilians, rhynchocephalians, and squamates. Students familiar with advances in phylogenetic systematics will recognize that *Reptilia* must biologically include birds and, according to some interpretations, mammals, in a comprehensive group called Amniota. It is not my intention in this section to cause taxonomic confusion for non-biologists, and I bring up this point only to clarify my usage of these terms for readers familiar with contemporary advances in systematics and nomenclature.

CRUSTACEANS

Crustaceans represent a subphylum of the more inclusive phylum Arthropoda, to which belong spiders, horseshoe crabs, scorpions, insects, crabs, shrimp, and lobsters, among others. The Crustacea include the latter three groups, and totals in excess of 40,000 named species, primarily marine in habitat. Despite this amazing diversity, there are relatively few freshwater taxa that become available to collectors.

Macrobrachium sp., from Costa Rica. Photo by Paul Freed.

Perhaps most familiar to aquarists is the group of decapods known as *crayfish*. In general usage, *crayfish* refers to a freshwater lobster, organisms with enlarged front claws for seizing and tearing prey. Crayfish are opportunistic feeders, taking any live prey that they can overpower, including most aquarium fish species. If you must mix crayfish with fishes, be sure the fishes are large, and the aquarium is large enough to allow fish to move away from crays. Even if the crayfish cannot overpower a fish, it may still cause injury through constant attacks.

In most cases, crayfish are retiring animals that need shelter during the day. Crays in nature are found under large, flat stones or sunken logs, and venture out in the dusk and dawn hours to feed. Though they will accept many conventional fish foods, particularly pellets

Macro-brachium niponensis. Photo by H. J. Richter.

Atydid shrimp. Photo by Guido Dingerkus.

be led to believe that your crayfish has died. If in doubt, check the water carefully—the soft-bodied cray is probably hiding during the few days it will take for the new exoskeleton to completely harden. Molts, however, should be removed promptly. Even the crayfish will not eat this material.

Crayfish have enlarged front pincers known as *chelipeds*, and with these may deliver a very painful pinch. The grip can be tenacious, though they usually pinch and release quickly.

Other commonly available crustaceans include freshwater shrimps, distinguished from crayfishes by the lack of enlarged chelipeds, presence of very long antennae, and in modifications of the mandibles. These animals are usually small, up to 2.5 in/6.3 cm in length, and include the familiar "see-through" glass shrimps. Unlike crays, shrimps are usually particle feeders, constantly shoveling soil into the mouth, extracting organic matter and regurgitating the soil. In many cases they will also act as scavengers, slowly picking apart the dead bodies of much larger organisms. Shrimp will routinely consume algae

and *Tubifex* worms, they will require small fishes, either alive or frozen. They will also consume fishes that die in the aquarium, and in this way may actually complement the filter system.

As a crayfish grows, its outer covering, the exoskeleton, will crack, and the animal will emerge from the old shell, leaving it in one piece. If you have never kept a crustacean alive before, the first time you see a molted skin you will growing in the substrate, but such algal growths are typical of established aquariums. If you must keep shrimp, allow the aquarium a few months to develop an algal coat in the substrate. Shrimp will also consume fish food that finds its way to the bottom and may even take brine shrimp on occasion.

Because shrimp are less able to defend themselves than crayfishes, many fish will attack them. To most fishes, the long, wormlike antennae and the rapidly moving swimmerets (modified appendages under the tail, used in locomotion) must appear as very enticing food items, and it is common to see shrimps with missing appendages. Larger fishes may even successfully remove a limb from a shrimp, if not eat it completely. The best fishes, then, to house with these odd animals, would be medium-sized schooling fishes, such as tetras, barbs, and rasboras.

One other very common freshwater crustacean is the *fiddler crab*, actually a large group of crabs wherein the males have one grotesquely enlarged cheliped that can be used to signal a warning, to stake a territory, or to attract a mate. Like crayfishes and shrimps,

Pacifastacus leniusculus, from Santa Cruz, California. Photo by Ken Lucas.

crabs are frequently terrestrial, and may spend most of their time out of the water (unlike crayfishes and shrimps). Nevertheless, they must be kept moist, and should not be housed in aquaterrariums with dry substrates on the terrestrial side. For most commonly available crab species, expect them to spend more time out of the water than in the water. When on land, crabs will often excavate a nearly vertical burrow into the sand, into which they can retreat with amazing rapidity when disturbed.

Crabs are, like shrimp, particle feeders and

Freshwater crabs are ideal critters for aquaterrarium occupancy, but be careful what you house them with—they are aggressive, opportunistic feeders, which means they'll attack whatever they think they'll be able to eat, and that certainly includes other creatures in the enclosure. Photo above (*Platytelphusa* sp., from Tanganyika), by Dr. Herbert R. Axelrod. Photo below (*Potamon* sp., from Thailand) by Aaron Norman.

scavengers, their large, pointed claws making disarticulation of carrion quite easy. In the water they are also formidable predators, and, like crayfishes, will readily consume any fish small enough to be overpowered. They, too, feed almost constantly, and a varied diet will be made of algae, fish flakes, small fish, *Tubifex* worms, and some decaying plant matter.

Crustaceans are extremely sensitive to certain metals, especially copper, in their environment, and even the presence of tiny quantities of these chemicals will prove lethal. The most typical source of introduced copper is in medicines used to treat some fish diseases. Be sure to check the label for drug constituents before adding them to an aquaterrarium that is home to crabs, shrimp, or crayfishes. Many flake foods for fishes contain excess copper and should be avoided.

FISHES

By far the largest group of vertebrate animals, fishes are among the most familiar pets in homes around the world. One source was quoted in the late 1960s as placing the aquarium hobby second only to photography in America. I am not sure that this ranking remains

One of the more appealing characteristics of freshwater crabs is the fact that many of them are strikingly colored and patterned. This specimen from southern Nicaragua, for example, is a truly beautiful animal. Photo by Don Conkel.

The best place to get ideas for your aquaterrarium setup is from the master source—nature itself. Shown is a place known to the author as "Frog Island." Photo by the author.

intact, but certainly the number of aquarists has grown, as reflected by the presence of an aquarium shop in almost every town, the number of aquarium-related magazines published, and the ever-growing volumes about aquaculture produced by major publishing houses. Fishes that were rare and exotic in 1960 are extensively bred today. Popular magazines have long run articles by psychologists touting aquariums as peace-inducing aspects of a home, providing a safer and more consistent aid to relaxation after a day of stress than can be offered by many drugs or forms of therapy. In fact, many health practitioners in stressful specialties that have highly stressful side-effects (e.g., dentists, surgeons, psychologists) have aquariums in their waiting rooms or offices. Consequently, the combination of approval from medical practitioners, psychologists, and the simple esthetic beauty of a well-kept aquarium, make it a popular and regular choice for pet keepers.

Tropical fishes, as broadly used, include standard aquarium species, even though many, such as Goldfish and White Cloud Mountain Minnows, are temperate in origin. They are divided into three categories based upon their water requirements: marine, brackish, and freshwater. Marine aquariums are very specialized environmental systems only suited for aquaterrariums in very large and, at this time, expensive enclosures. Brackish systems are somewhat less demanding, and can be briefly lumped for our purposes with freshwater systems.

A few pointers on purchasing fishes. First, remember that oxygen content of aquarium water is limited more than it would be in nature, and that warm water, necessary for tropical fishes, carries less dissolved oxygen than cooler water. Combine this with the fact that freshwater fishes tend to be constantly dumping nitrogenous wastes into the water, and you can see how quickly an aquarium can be loaded beyond its carrying capacity (or the number of organisms that can be housed and kept alive in the aquarium).

Let us suppose that you have a 10-gallon water section in your aquaterrarium. According to most estimates, this allows you room to safely keep ten fishes, each up to 1 in/2.5 cm in length. If you were to add all these fish at once to a new aquarium, chances are most or all would die within days. Why? For several reasons, two of particular importance. First, new water (having had no fish or other organisms in it before) will be devoid of denitrifying bacteria. These bacteria build in population size if there is enough organic

Cardinal Tetras, *Para-cheirodon axelrodi*. Photo by M. P. and C. Piednoir.

waste matter for them to feed upon. They enter the aquarium system as passengers in new fish and in the water brought from a pet shop. By adding, say, ten fish to a bacteria-limited aquarium, the fishes will produce toxic, nitrogenous wastes (such as lethal ammonia) faster than bacteria can detoxify them.

If instead you added three fish to start the aquarium, within ten to 14 days the bacterial levels should be high enough to accommodate the three fishes safely, and make it possible to add another one or two new fishes. However, at no point should you increase a population by a large number of fishes at once.

The other major concern deals with fish health. Animals with fluctuating body temperatures, such as fishes, are extremely susceptible to stress-induced illnesses. A purchased fish is subjected to the stress of (1) being chased around its

Oscar, *Astronotus ocellatus.* Photo by Dr. Warren E. Burgess.

Neon Tetras, *Para-cheirodon innesi.* Photo by Mark Smith.

aquarium by a pet shop employee, (2) being netted, (3) being pulled out of the water, (4) subjected to the confines of a plastic bag, and (5) the violent motions involved while the bag is in transport, along with (6) temperature fluctuations in your automobile, either warmer or cooler than the aquarium was, only to be (7) released in a new tank with at least slightly, often considerably different, water conditions, including variation in temperature, hardness, nitrogenous waste levels, and pH. Any one of these factors is enough to cause some metabolic imbalance to begin, allowing a bacterial or viral infection to overpower the fish, which in turn becomes a possible source of infection to other fishes in the aquarium. Buying one or two fishes at a time eases stress on the animals because you are better able to observe them for signs of illness. Making corrections for one fish is much easier and cost effective than trying to treat an entire aquarium community. The sick fish can be removed and treated in isolation, often with better results than dosing an entire community for a week.

Because of the broad variety of living fishes available to even the most novice aquarist, I shall not go into the details of each

There are a few commercially produced turtle foods available to the keeper. Most are highly nutritious and can be used as the staple item. Photo courtesy Wardley.

possibility in this volume, recommending that the reader should both peruse the local aquarium shops and the T.F.H. books mentioned earlier in this text. From these sources you can quickly glean ideas about what types of fishes you wish to keep, be it schools of small colorful tetras, or a few large and formidable cichlids. In the sections following I would like to present a brief resume of those species of particular suitability to the aquaterrarium.

Foremost among these fishes must be the mudskippers, of the family Periophthalmidae. These are estuarine fish that are widely distributed in the southern tropics of the Old World. They are all brackish water fishes,

requiring some salt in the aquarium water. I should add here that brackish water fishes require commercially available sea salt mixtures in the water, not table salt (yes, I have known many people who use table salt), and added at about one quarter to one fifth the amount needed for a strictly marine aquarium. This will, of course, limit the selection of other species you may add to the aquaterrarium to other estuarine dwellers, including puffers, scats, monos, and flounders, to name those most frequently encountered. Many livebearers and some cichlids tolerate brackish water very well, too.

Mudskippers are peculiar fishes, and may be easily mistaken, at first glance,

Mudskippers (*Perioph-thalmus* sp.) are fascinating aquaterrarium subjects. Hardy and unique-looking, many people mistake them for some strange variety of salamander. Photo by the author.

Fishkeepers needn't worry about acquiring proper foods for their pets—there are many available. Check a reliable guide to see what your particular animals eat, then travel to your local pet shop to obtain the item or items required. Many can be bought frozen and in bulk. Photo courtesy of Ocean Nutrition.

for some elongate, bug-eyed salamander. The high, blunt head, cylindrical body and forearm-like pectoral fins all combine to make these animals look like some transition species between fish and amphibian. In fact, however, mudskippers are quite firmly placed in the class of bony fishes, and though preferring to spend communities that could be fairly described as swarms, with thousands occupying even a small region of mangrove beach. They are extremely opportunistic feeders, consuming everything smaller than themselves that they can find, from insects and small crustaceans to other fishes. These versatile fishes are capable of rapid

Although they act more like amphibians than fishes, mudskippers do indeed belong to the latter group. Like most fishes, they cannot stay out of water indefinitely. Photo by Heinrich Stulz.

most of their time out of water (like fiddler crabs), must stay near enough to water to keep moist and to replenish water as it is lost. In much the same way that a human can take an air supply underwater in SCUBA tanks, mudskippers bring a water supply on land in the spaces underlying the comparatively huge opercula, or gill covers, at the back of the head.

Mudskippers may live in pursuit, and may even climb trees and bushes in pursuit of prey.

However adroit they appear, mudskippers are rather defenseless when on land, and their safety is due largely to the softness of the sands they frequent. Large predators have difficulty moving over such wet, loose substrate. When the

tide comes in, mudskippers often retreat into burrows until the tide again recedes. Apparently, the adaptations that make mudskippers so successful on land have put them at a disadvantage in the water, where they would be easy prey for numerous predatory species of more conventional fishes.

Another odd group that would do well in a freshwater aquaterrarium is the superorder Dipnoi, or lungfishes. The few living species are known from Africa, South America, and Australia, but it is from the first two continents that most aquarium specimens will be obtained. The special claim to fame of this group is based on the ability of African and South American species to live for months at a time out of water. As drought dries standing bodies of water, these elongate, eel-like fishes burrow into the soft mud. There they envelop themselves in a sticky, spheroid cocoon, to which surrounding mud particles will adhere. As the lake or pond dries, this ball, too, dries and hardens. The fish within enters a state of torpor which may last for

Left: Keeping an eye on the pH level in your tank is very important, especially where certain delicate fish species are concerned. If you can get a hold of a buffer that will help you maintain the proper levels, do so. Photo courtesy of Fritz Chemical Company. **Below:** South American Lungfish, *Lepidosiren*.

Photo by Edward C. Taylor.

Since there are so very many commercially produced fish foods, a keeper should have no excuse for not be able to provide his or her fishes with a steady supply of foodstuffs. Many of these products are truly excellent. Photo courtesy of Hagen.

several years. When rain refills the lake, the cocoon softens, and the lungfish emerges intact, ready to resume life where it left off long ago.

Lungfishes are not always available on the pet market, and when they are for sale may vary tremendously in price. Part of this stems from the fact that lungfishes are not yet being commercially bred, and part from the fact they originate in countries that often make collecting and export difficult.

Both African and South American lungfishes may exceed three feet in total length, though aquarium specimens are usually in the 4-9 inch size range. Unlike mudskippers, they will not venture out of the water, nor are they very active fishes. From time to

time they can be observed swimming to the surface to get a gulp of air, then they return to the bottom. They are strong predators, and employ the sit-and-wait strategy of letting prey come to them. The jaws are large and strong, and lungfishes will make a fast meal out of other fishes and amphibians. Consequently, they should not be housed with other animals small enough to make a meal.

A fish that can truly shine in an aquaterrarium is the archer fish, *Toxotes jaculator*, found from the Red Sea east to Indonesia. This adaptable species can survive in marine, brackish, or fresh water, though aquarists tell me that best results are obtained in a brackish water aquarium. A typical aquarium specimen will measure 3-5 inches in length, and will be a surface swimmer.

The archer fish is well known for its habit of spotting invertebrate prey above the water—including spiders in webs, mosquitoes in flight, and beetles on tree limbs—and shooting a stream of water from its mouth to knock the prey down to the fish below. The aim of the fish is remarkably accurate, especially when you consider that it must account for diffraction of light rays entering the water. But these amazing fish are not limited to prey that they shoot with water, and they will readily consume pellet food as well as the standard live and frozen aquarium standards.

If the idea of a fish wandering around on land is what inspires you, mudskippers need not be your only choice (unless you live in one of those states, such as California or Florida, where this next species is prohibited). The walking catfish, *Clarias batrachus*, regularly comes ashore, and can traverse several miles moving from one body of water to another, all overland. It is unusual in being commonly found in nature as an albino, and this color form is more popular with aquarists than the brown

Archer fish, *Toxotes chatareus*. Photo by M. P. and C. Piednoir.

Archer fish, *Toxotes chatareus*. Photo by Dr. Herbert R. Axelrod.

and tan morph. *Clarias* catfishes are widely distributed in Africa and southern Asia, and have become introduced to areas of Florida and, possibly, elsewhere.

These are large mouthed catfishes with equally large appetites, which makes them serious competitors for food in an aquarium or a lake. They are predatory, taking other fishes, crustaceans, insects, and some molluscs. Like the mudskipper, they retain water over the gills by securing the operculum shut while on land. Their ability to breathe air makes it possible for *Clarias* to survive in stagnant, oxygen-poor water that would be quite lethal to other fishes. When the water becomes too stagnant, it is thought, the walking catfish becomes amphibian and leaves the water to search for a more suitable new home.

Aquaterrarists should note that a walking catfish on land may overpower and consumer terrestrial residents of the container, including frogs and small lizards.

The nature of an aquaterrarium allows combinations of fish species that might not work so well in a conventional aquarium. For example, if you have a sloped shoreline to which rocks have been glued, you are providing a shallow water area with small refuges for tiny

Walking Catfish, *Clarias batrachus*. Photo by Ken Lucas.

Once a health problem with your fishes begins, you must deal with it immediately. Shown are two products that will help you. These are available at many pet shops. Photo courtesy of Aquarium Products, Inc.

fishes, such as guppies, while simultaneously having open, deeper water for larger fishes that would normally consume the small ones. I have seen one remarkable example of this design that contained a 25-gallon aquatic area, in which there were two shallow water species (guppies and a killifish) under 2 inches in length, while nearby swam a school of 6-inch iridescent sharks (*Pangasius sutchi*). As a shark approached a smaller fish, the latter would dash between the small rocks of the shoreline, into water too shallow for *Pangasius* to follow. In this way, three species of schooling fish were housed together, the large *Pangasius* providing a true show fish, the smaller species giving a realistic sense of streamside life upon close inspection of the vivarium. True, some smaller fishes did fall prey to the larger ones, but this had been part of the intent.

In an aquaterrarium such as that just described, embellishments can be added to further enhance the naturalness of the environment. Large, bushy aquatic plants, such as *Labomba* and *Ceratopteris*, lined along the rear wall of the aquarium, provide a sort of buffer between shallow water and open water species, and may enable the smaller species to expand their swimming area considerably. The addition of such cover makes the likelihood that the smaller livebearers can successfully reproduce. I have raised numerous generations of guppies and mollies in such aquaterraria, with considerable success. Some fry are eaten by larger fishes, but the survival rate is slightly more favorable than the normal ecological balance rate (which is about one

Iridescent Shark, *Pangasius sutchi*. Photo by M. P. and C. Piednoir.

offspring per set of parents).

As a showpiece, the aquaterrarium will be less dependent upon its animals than its plants. Nevertheless, animals that are conspicuous are part of the reason for building such a unit. Schools of small fishes may look great in a standard aquarium or a small aquaterrarium, but the larger versions will be enhanced by larger species of fishes. I have already mentioned the beautiful *Pangasius* sp. Other hardy candidates include Congo tetras (*Phenacogrammus interruptus*), tricolor sharks (*Balantiocheilus melanopterus*), Australian rainbowfishes (*Melanotaenia* species), Celebes rainbowfishes (*Telmatherina ladigesi*), tiger barbs (*Capoeta tetrazona*), and danios (*Danio* species), to name a few. Most all of these species exceed 4 inches in total length, swim in schools, and display interesting and conspicuous colors. They all accept flake and frozen foods, and thrive in a standard tropical fish tank temperature range (68-75°F), so they provide no real feeding or maintenance problems. If you elect to go with any of these species, remember the caveat above: *don't add the whole school at one time, but rather add one or two fish to the aquarium and allow about two weeks*

Congo Tetra, *Phenaco-grammus interruptus*. Photo by Mark Smith.

Tricolor Shark, *Balantiocheilos melanopterus*. Photo by M. P. and C. Piednoir.

Catfish, *Clarias* sp. Photo by Dr. Herbert R. Axelrod.

Above: Tiger Barbs, *Capoeta tetrazona.* Photo by M. P. and C. Piednoir.

Right: Giant Danio, *Danio malabaricus.* Photo by B. Kahl.

before the next introduction. Overcrowding and addition of too many fish at one time probably rank with overfeeding as the major causes of premature tropical fish mortality.

AMPHIBIANS

In many cases, amphibians are the aquatic component of the aquaterrarium, for most species will readily move back and forth between land and water while a great many species are totally or primarily aquatic. But it would be wrong to think of amphibians merely as modified fishes, at least so far as husbandry is concerned,

for they differ from fishes in several ways.

While many fish are marine or estuary dwellers, only a few frog species can tolerate exposure to saltwater (one being the Crab-eating Frog, *Rana cancivora*). Even low concentrations of salt can be lethal to an overwhelming majority of amphibians. This is all related to that high school biology subtopic of osmosis. Freshwater fishes and amphibians have blood that is hypertonic to the water outside the body, which means that the animal is constantly absorbing water which must be as rapidly excreted lest the animal swell and burst. If exposed to saltwater, the rate of fluid excretion is greatly increased, causing the animal to shrivel and desiccate.

While many amphibians have evolved adaptations to survive in some of the world's most formidable deserts, these species are not candidates for the aquaterrarium. The species for this environment are those from rain and temperature forests, and includes the majority of known species. Few will do well on a substrate of wood or gravel. Wood is abrasive, and may easily injure smooth amphibian skin. Others will burrow, an activity frustrated by gravel. Thus the substrate of choice is potting soil.

Living amphibians fall into three orders, each having representatives available to the aquaterrarist.

Caecilians

This is a remarkable group of limbless, often tailless, worm-like amphibians. They live in the tropics of South America, Africa, and Asia, but are very secretive and rarely encountered. About 160 species have been described, making caecilians the smallest group of living amphibians.

Among their unusual features are small scales beneath the skin of the body, and sensory tentacles that can be extended from apertures between the eye and the mouth. This tentacle is attached to the olfactory nerve, and serves as an enhanced odor detecting organ. Two species are frequently found for sale.

The Common Aquatic Caecilian, *Typhlonectes natans*, is a blue-black, rubbery looking animal that grows to about 13 in/ 33 cm. Pet shops usually sell them as *rubber eels*, or as some corruption of the

Common Aquatic Caecilian, *Typhlonectes natans*. All photos by Dr. Warren E. Burgess.

Common Aquatic Caecilian, *Typhlonectes natans*. Photo by the author.

word *caecilian*. The tiny eyes are covered by skin, making the animal blind (*caecilian* is from the Greek for *blind ones*). The tail is absent, an the body terminates in a ring that contains the cloaca.

Aquatic caecilians are capable of surviving on land for extended periods of time. They mate by bringing the cloacae in contact while the male transfers sperm to the female. Gestation takes about six months, the female retaining the developing young in her body. Up to five young are

Common Aquatic Caecilian, *Typhlonectes natans*. Neonate showing gill membrane. Photo by R. D. Bartlett.

Argentine Caecilian, *Chthonerpeton vivipararum*, feeding on an earthworm. Photo by J. Visser.

born alive and lack the large external gills common to other neonate caecilians. These animals are carnivorous and will accept chopped earthworms, bloodworms, *Tubifex*, and small pieces of meat.

The other common caecilian available to herpetoculturists is the southeast Asian *Ichthyophis glutinosus*, or Yellow-striped Caecilian. This handsome species grows to at least 18 in/ 45.7 cm, and can live in an aquarium or terrarium, making it ideal for the aquaterrarium. Slate gray above, it has a bright yellow stripe down either side that meets or just barely meets along the belly. Like *Typhlonectes*, *Ichthyophis* has concealed, virtually useless eyes.

Yellow-striped Caecilians have rarely bred in captivity, and much of what we know about their reproductive biology is based on museum specimens. Females lay a cluster of eggs under a moist log or rock, or in a deep burrow, and she wraps herself around them until they hatch.

These inoffensive amphibians will feed on

insects, such as mealworms, waxworms, and blood worms, and will take freshly killed crickets. They barely move fast enough to capture a living cricket. If they are kept on a soil substrate they will spend most of their time buried. Apparently, they have acute senses of hearing, or at least of detecting vibrations, for they are quick to surface once live insects are added to the aquaterrarium. Specimens I have housed with Chinese crocodile lizards are often hidden under bark for days at a time but emerge within a minute or so after I introduce crickets or wax worms to the terrarium. The caecilians will frequently accept food offered by hand, and this may be the best way to ensure that new arrivals are, in fact, feeding regularly.

Salamanders

Salamanders number only about twice as many species as caecilians, with about 360 described to date, but they are much more familiar to people around the world than the last group. For one thing, salamanders live in places frequented by man, including most of the tropical and temperate world, excluding most of Africa, India, and Australasia. Species diversity reaches its zenith in the eastern United States, where most of the lungless and mole salamanders are to be found. Though they are often collected in very warm tropical habitats,

Fire Salamanders, *Salamandra salamandra*. These are among the hardiest of all salamander pets. Photo by the author.

Palmate Newts, *Triturus helveticus*. Photo by L. Wischnath.

salamanders require moist conditions in captivity, and rarely tolerate a temperature above 75°F. Many rugged species, such as the Crocodile Newt, *Tylototriton verrucosus,* can withstand temperatures in excess of 80°F, but most species will refuse to feed above a particular critical temperature. The rule of thumb of salamanders (remembering that there are, alas, always exceptions) is keep them cool—between 60 and 70°F.

Most salamanders resemble lizards: the body is elongate and cylindrical, there are four limbs and clearly defined digits (usually), and a distinct tail. Salamanders typically have bulging, frog-like eyes. The skin lacks scales and is full of mucous glands which give the animal a slimy covering. The toes never bear claws, the front limb ends in four or fewer fingers, and there is no external ear, as is seen in most lizards. Many salamanders can exceed the regenerative powers of lizards, for a lizard can only regrow a lost tail (only in some species, and then only imperfectly), while a salamander can regenerate an entire leg, bones and all.

Salamanders (and the primarily aquatic forms, called *newts*), are all carnivorous and require live foods. Most are secretive and will spend months at a time buried in moist soil. In contrast, aquatic species, including most newts, axolotls, and mudpuppies, are fairly active animals, some with bright colors, and may make better exhibit animals than many terrestrial salamanders.

Mudpuppies and waterdogs (genus *Necturus*) have long been used in biology labs as dissection specimens and have only recently become more or less common as pets. These are large salamanders, growing to over 12 in/30.4 cm, that retain aquatic features throughout their lives. Most conspicuous is the pair of long, bushy gills that jut out from the rear of the skull. In warm, oxygen-poor water, the gills are pulsed and become bright red in color. Conversely, in cool, oxygen-rich water, the gills are a somber maroon, held close together and near the body. The retention of juvenile characters is known as *paedomorphosis*, and implies that the amphibian becomes sexually mature without completely leaving the larval stage.

Mudpuppies, due to their large size, can deliver a painful bite, but only do so if securely grasped. If you have ever tried to seize

Alpine Newt, *Triturus alpestris*. Photo by R. Guyetant.

Below: Crested Newt, *Triturus cristatus*. Showing belly pattern of adult. Photo by Michael Gilroy.

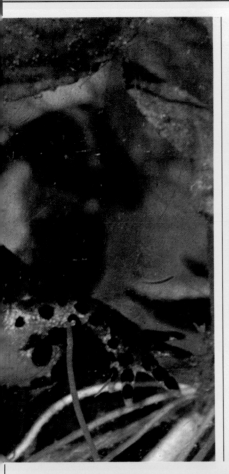

a mudpuppy, you know how unlikely a task you chose, for they are among the slimiest of creatures. Normally, they must be netted in order to be transported.

The giant salamanders of China and Japan (genus *Andrias*) are truly giant by amphibian standards, growing to 5 ft/130 cm or more in length. These bizarre animals are also paedomorphic, but lack the flowing gills of mudpuppies. They are truly odd-looking creatures, with a broad, flat head, short stumpy tail, and tiny eyes that are hard to see for all the skin folds on the head. These long-lived giants have been recorded as surviving in captivity for over 50 years.

Crested Newt, *Triturus cristatus*. Larva feeding from worm cup. Photo by Michael Gilroy.

Arizona Tiger Salamander, *Ambystoma tigrinum nebulosum*. Larval specimen. Photo by W. P. Mara.

Mole salamanders (of the Ambystomatidae) are particularly abundant in eastern United States forests, though they are generally secretive and found above ground only during the early spring rains. At these times, the burrowing salamanders emerge from a fossorial existence in search of ponds where they will find a mate, reproduce, and

Chinese Giant Salamander, *Andrias davidianus*. Photo by the author.

spend a brief time foraging for food before returning to the underground world. This tendency towards secretiveness makes most mole salamanders poor exhibit animals, (though a few larger species actually do quite well in the during daylight hours. Tiger Salamanders are so named because of the pattern, but it could well apply to their feeding habits as well for they are voracious eaters, consuming anything they can swallow. I once kept

terrarium).

Most popular of the ambystomatids is the wide-ranging Tiger Salamander, *Ambystoma tigrinum,* which is found throughout the U.S. and southern Canada in all but the truly arid, desert habitats. This black and yellow-barred species may grow to over 10 in/25 cm in length, and will often take to the water an adult Tiger Salamander in an aquaterrarium with a small water snake. One day, the salamander ate the snake, which was a good 4 in/10 cm longer than the amphibian. Alas, the meal was too much, and a few days later the salamander died. But this serves as a good indicator about how aggressive these salamanders can be;

Eastern Tiger Salamander, *Ambystoma tigrinum tigrinum.* Photo by R. T. Zappalorti.

they should not be housed with smaller species.

As with most terrestrial salamanders, Tiger Salamanders are not particularly adroit, and though they can eat crickets, they have great difficulty capturing swifter insects. Foods should therefore include various worms, mealworms, and

striking in comparing the American Tiger Salamander to the European Fire Salamander, *Salamandra salamandra*. Here is another large (10 to 12 in/ 25.4 to 30.4 cm), black and yellow spotted terrestrial species. Unlike mole salamanders, Fire Salamanders do not spend much time underground,

Southern Redback Salamander, *Plethodon serratus*. Photo by R. D. Bartlett.

waxworms. Mole salamanders will readily accept pieces of meat offered by hand or at the tip of a slender stick.

The Old World salamanders (family Salamandridae) are similar in appearance to the mole salamanders. This convergence is particularly

but instead come out at night, particularly during rains, to search for food. This species is especially cold tolerant and only seeks a hibernaculum during the very coldest days of winter. Fire Salamanders are often seen wandering across snow or wading in near-freezing streams. Like their New World counterparts, Fire Salamanders will consume anything large enough to be overpowered, including small rodents and fledgling birds.

Lungless salamanders (family Plethodontidae) are similar in appearance to mole salamanders, and both live in much the same geographic area, though requires lungless salamanders to keep their skin moist at all times, so many species live in streams or splash zones near moving water. Others live under leaf litter, where humidity levels are high enough to keep the skin moist. This lunglessness coupled with a terrestrial mode of life severely restricts the maximum size

Redback Salamander, *Plethodon cinereus*. Photo by Guido Dingerkus.

plethodontids extend further south into Central and South America. Lungless salamanders can be recognized by the groove extending from the nostril straight down to the upper jaw. Of course, members of this family lack lungs in the adult form. All respiration is through skin. Such cutaneous respiration attainable by plethodontids, the largest only about 8 in/20.3 cm in total length. Nevertheless, lungless salamanders are the most numerous, in terms of species, of all salamanders.

Familiar to many residents of the eastern United States is the tiny Redback Salamander,

Facing page: Tiger Salamander, *Ambystoma tigrinum*, feeding on a mouse. Photo by K. T. Nemuras.

Arboreal Salamander, *Aneides lugubris*. Specimen from the San Francisco Bay area. Photo by Dr. Sherman A. Minton.

Plethodon cinereus, which grows to 4.5 in/11.4 cm long. This widespread species lives under leaf litter in a variety of habitats, from dandy loam to dark soil. Though commonly found near streams, they are not restricted to such localities, and I have collected specimens a considerable distance from the nearest standing water. Though common, their ecology is very poorly known, and I am unaware of any report of observations of eggs in the wild, though related species do tend nests. Young specimens undergo the larval stage in the egg, so they hatch as tiny versions of the adults.

Redback Salamanders occur in two color varieties, the red-backed (red stripe down back, body slate gray) and lead-backed (basically a uniform gray), both of which are randomly distributed in the same basic range. These tiny species rarely enter the water, will spend most of their time hidden, and require a diet of tiny invertebrates, including small mealworms and baby crickets.

Quite different is the West Coast's Arboreal Salamander, *Aneides lugubris*. Growing to 7 in/ 17.7 cm, it is a larger bodied species than the much more slender Redback Salamander. This is a ghostly looking animal, with a pale pinkish or grayish color lacking any pattern. The toes are square in appearance, and the tail

much shorter, comparatively, than in other lungless species.

Like its eastern counterpart, the arboreal salamander is found in a variety of habitats, provided there are moist refugia, or places where humidity is high enough to keep the skin moist. Though they are expert climbers, often found in trees, they are as often seen under fallen logs and large rocks. In the aquaterrarium they are inclined to spend considerable time in the water. The diet includes all manner of small insects and worms.

Perhaps the most versatile species for the aquaterrarium are the newts. These are salamanders that, upon hatching from an aquatic egg, undergo a tadpole-like larval stage. As the newt matures, it leaves the water for a period of time, becoming a terrestrial eft. As they become sexually mature, the efts return to the water, and may sport a crest along the back, a fin around the tail, and may even change color drastically from the eft hues.

Pet shops frequently have several newts for sale. Most common is probably the Eastern Newt, *Notophthalmus viridescens*. Adults are olive green, with black-bordered orange dorsal spots and a yellow belly. Males have a conspicuous fin along the upper and lower surfaces of the tail during the mating

"Red eft" stage of the Red-spotted Newt, *Notophthalmus viridescens viridescens*. Photo by William B. Allen, Jr.

season. The terrestrial stage is known as the red eft, where the dorsum is orange instead of olive and the tail lacks fins. These are small salamanders, rarely exceeding 3 in/7.6 cm in length, and will spend most of their time in the water (efts are rarely available from commercial sources; if you want them, you will have to breed the newts and raise them yourself). They will take a

provide some sort of water flow effect. This handsome species is black above, but has a bright orange-red underside. When intimidated, they arch the head and tail to expose the bright belly colors. In nature, red is a warning color, usually signifying that the owner possesses a powerful toxin. This should be a warning to herpetoculturists, for *Taricha* has the same toxin

Broken-striped Newt, *Notophthalmus viridescens dorsalis*. Photo by Mervin F. Roberts.

variety of fish foods, including some flakes and freeze-dried brine shrimp, but also require occasional feedings of live *Tubifex*, young crickets, small waxworms, or fruitflies.

Another western American species is the Red-bellied Newt, *Taricha rivularis*, apparently bred with considerable success by commercial fish breeders. They live in and around cool, fast-moving streams, so the aquarium should be well aerated to

found in poisonous pufferfishes, called tetradontotoxin, which is an extremely virulent nerve poison. Newspaper stories and herpetological beer-party legends to the contrary, ingesting one of these newts is very likely to prove lethal (for which reason you should avoid handling these animals, so wash thoroughly after you do handle them and abstain from keeping them if you have small children around the house).

Red-bellied Newts are hardy animals that may live for a decade or more, and they tend to be more active than either mole or lungless salamanders. Unlike many other newts, this species will spend as much time on land as in the water, and is among the more active of salamanders. Unlike other newts, these prefer slow-moving streams and the still water of clean lakes and ponds. They, too, have a powerful toxin secreted by skin glands, and should be handled only when necessary. The skin is more warty in texture than the Red-bellied Newt, and the undersurfaces are yellowish to pale orange. Otherwise, care is similar to that for the Red-bellied Newt.

A closely related species is the Rough-skinned Newt, *Taricha granulosa*, found over much of the western coast of the United States, from central California north through much of the Pacific Northwest into southern Alaska.

One of the most striking aquaterrarium animals to become available on the market in recent years has been the Crocodile Newt, also called Emperor, or Mandarin, Salamander, *Tylototriton verrucosus*, from central Asia. This animal has a dark skin covered with enlarged, orange tubercules, which form a U-shaped crest along the upper surface of the head. They are flat-bodied, but otherwise very newt-like in appearance, having rough rather than slimy skin. Growing to about 7 in/17.7 cm, this hardy species differs from other newts in being a poor swimmer, entering water only at the breeding time. Otherwise, it is a terrestrial animal, needing moist soil and plenty of hiding places. It is an active hunter, taking mealworms, waxworms, small bloodworms, and other soft-bodied prey.

Crocodile Newts are crepuscular (active at dawn and dusk), but make occasional daylight appearances.

Frogs and Toads

As successful and diverse as the salamanders may be, the great amphibian success story must be that of the anurans, or, frogs and toads. A cosmopolitan group showing incredible diversity of form and habits, they include over 3,400 described species, and are absent only from Antarctica, the far North, and much of Saharan Africa. Among amphibians, it is the anurans that have penetrated the harshest

Facing page: Red eft stage of the Red-spotted Newt, *Notophthalmus viridescens viridescens.* Photo by Dr. Sherman A. Minton.

Mandarin Salamander, *Tylototriton verrucosus*. Photo by the author.

Facing page: Rough-skinned Newt, *Taricha granulosa*. Photo by H. Hansen.

special canals and nerves to control balance; hearing is a beneficial by-product of ear development.

Frogs also had the first truly extensible tongue, which is used as a prey-grasping organ. But the tongue has virtually no ability to manipulate food in the mouth, so swallowing is aided by pushing down and back with the undersides of the eyeballs. Watch a frog eat, and you will see the grimace as it swallows. This facial expression is not a sign of disgust (at least, I am assuming that frogs do not actually think 'yuck, another worm!', or anything else for that matter!), but a functional and necessary part of the swallowing process.

A feature unique to anurans (which, by the way means *tail-less*), is the fused vertebral structure, called a *urostyle*. No other animal group has this unusual character. Many species have greatly elongated hind legs, which are used to allow a frog to leap. These limbs, however, can be quite short in many species of toads and the aforementioned desert

deserts, some species living well below the searing sandy surface in a self-made cocoon. Others frequent the canopy level of the world's tropical forests, giving themselves a varnish, spreading waxy substances over the skin to retard water loss.

Frogs combine an interesting array of derived features. They are possibly the first vertebrates to develop a true voice, and with that acquisition came the first hearing ear. The inner ear, found in various forms in other amphibians and some fishes, is essentially an organ for balance. Even your human ear is largely made up of

frogs, but they retain a characteristic position, recalling a runner's crouch.

The terms *frog* and *toad* are often interchangeable. *Frog* usually refers to a smooth-skinned, long-legged, largely aquatic

informal survey suggests that frogs are probably the best-studied group of herptiles, snakes coming in a somewhat distant second. True or not, herpetologists have conducted extensive and impressive studies on frogs

A fairly typical ranid frog, *Rana esculenta*. Photo by M. P. and C. Piednoir.

anuran. In contrast, *toads* are warty, with short hind limbs, and are primarily terrestrial in habits. But the biologist's caveat remains intact for this group since there are always exceptions.

Anurans are the best-studied living amphibians, and herpetologists who study anuran biology are active in most of the world's major museums and universities. An

around the world, and even a few of the remotest countries have field guides to the anuran fauna. Fortunately for herpetoculturists, this has made a great deal of useful data available for the improvement of husbandry, and many species of very exotic frogs are currently being bred with regularity equaled only by tropical fish and bird breeders.

The aquaterrarium is a special environment, capable of sustaining a great variety of animals and plants, as should already be clear. Personally, I think the ultimate aquaterrarium contains large schooling fish, colorful treefrogs, active lizards, and a variety of orchids. It is no exaggeration to state that many tropical frogs will rival the most exquisite orchids in color and beauty.

Some frogs are so endowed with color that, when seen on a plain background, they are quite gaudy, the colors almost harsh to observe. Put that same frog in a paludarium with vines and flowers simulating its natural habitat and it becomes an intricate, even subtle, part of the overall picture. Such a species that immediately

Red-eyed Treefrog, *Agalychnis callidryas*. This frog needs humidity and plenty of land space for hunting (which it does at night). Photo by Robert S. Simmons.

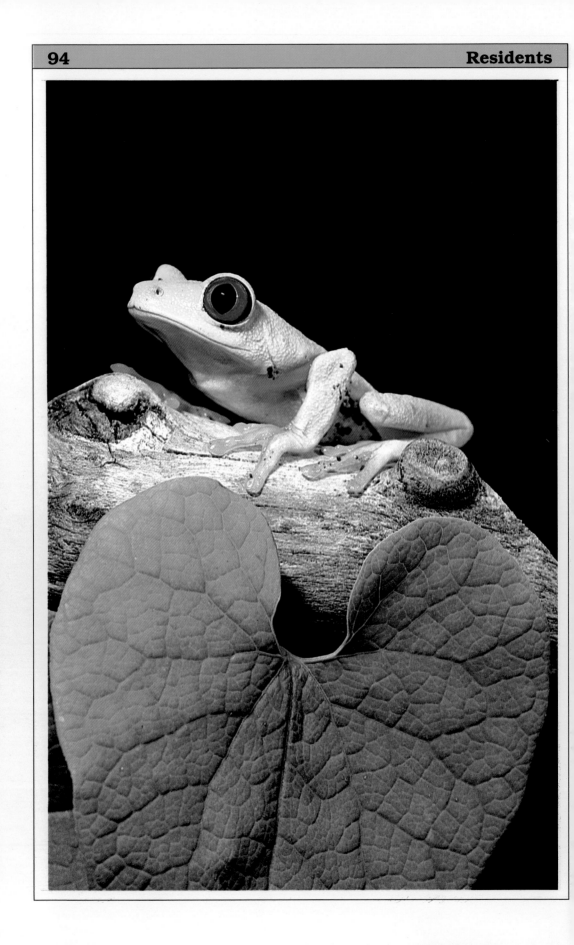

comes to mind is the Red-eyed Treefrog, *Agalychnis callidryas*. This beautiful frog comes from the high-humidity forests of Central America where it dwells among the epiphytes far above the ground. Captives must be kept in a moist environment, sprayed 2 to 3 times daily, and humidity kept above 70%. They are hunters, active at night, and will take a variety of insect foods, including crickets, flies, beetles, moths, and waxworms. They rarely come to the ground, so insects offered should be able to climb well. Red-eyed treefrogs can be housed with many of the salamanders and newts already mentioned, plus many other treefrog species, but are delicate animals that would not thrive if kept with active lizards.

Other, more common treefrogs include the Green and Gray Treefrogs, *Hyla cinerea* and *Hyla versicolor*, both common to the eastern United States. The Green Treefrog, found throughout the southeast, is normally a green animal with a cream stripe along each flank. On occasion, it can turn a darker color. This is a small species, under 3 in/7.6 cm, usually closer to 1.5 in/ 3.8 cm in total length, that inhabits places near still water, such as ponds and

Facing page: Most Red-eyed Treefrogs, *Agalychnis callidryas,* are fairly hardy in captivity, but a keeper must keep a close eye on their climatic requirements. They are very sensitive to improper environment. Photo by Michael Gilroy.

The popular and hardy Green Treefrog, *Hyla cinerea.* Photo by R. T. Zappalorti.

lakes. By day they are secreted under leaves or in logs near the water. At night, they forage in shallow water for small animals, such as mosquito larvae and *Daphnia*, that make up their diet.

The Gray Treefrog is found across most of the eastern half of the U.S. and just into adjacent Canada. It is less aquatic than the Green Treefrog, spending much of its time in logs or on trees, but still in the vicinity of still ponds. Both species are nocturnal, and will thrive in a vivarium with other small frogs, most newts, and small, diurnal lizards.

The true frogs, family Ranidae, include many standbys of the aquaterrarium, including the Green Frog, *Rana clamitans*, Leopard Frogs, *Rana pipiens*, and relatives, and the African Bullfrog, *Pyxicephalus adspersus*.

The Green Frog is a variable species, ranging in color from brown through green, with a few large, black spots across the posterior half of the body The ear in males is tremendous, far larger than the eye. This species ranges across much the same area as the Gray Treefrog, but is an aquatic animal, frequenting the shorelines of ponds and lakes. It is largely nocturnal, but may spend the day on logs, rocks, or grassy hillocks

Gray Treefrog, *Hyla versicolor*, from Michigan. Photo by R. T. Zappalorti.

overlooking the water. As you walk along a lakeside, the first hint that Green Frogs are present may be the plopping sound made as they leap into the water.

Leopard frogs turned into something of a surprise for biologists in the 1970s. This is the familiar species dissected in almost every high school and college in the United States, but immunological studies showed populations to be biochemically distinct.

Such species, that cannot be separated by observing external characters, are known as *cryptic species*. Today, authorities recognize at least 11 species of leopard frogs, from Canada south to central Mexico. Leopard frogs are found in many more habitats that Green Frogs, from near desert to mountains, yet are still closely tied to bodies of fresh water. Husbandry for both types of frog is similar. They eat a variety of live

Western Chorus Frog, *Pseudacris triseriata*. An excellent aqua-terrarium subject that can be housed and fed much like the Leopard Frogs. Photo of a Kansas specimen by R.T. Zappalorti.

The attractive and hardy Pickerel Frog, *Rana palustris*. This species should not be housed with other species due to the toxicity of its skin secretions. Photo by R. D. Bartlett.

foods, including insects, spiders, crustaceans (e.g., glass shrimp), and small fishes. These are swift, aggressive feeders and may be safely housed with most larger salamander species, medium-sized lizards, and many kinds of turtle.

Similar in appearance to leopard frogs is the Pickerel Frog, *Rana palustris*. This is a brown species with a paired series of dark, rectangular markings down the back. The skin secretions of this species produce some nasty poisons that will kill many other animals, including other frogs, on contact. Consequently, this look-alike should not be kept in an aquaterrarium with other species.

Quite a different ranid is the African Bullfrog, *Pyxicephalus adspersa*. Young frogs, around 4 in/ 10.1 cm long, that are rotund creatures, and walkers, not leapers. They are voracious eating machines, consuming anything moving that they can swallow. This leads to an obese adult frog, barely able to move about. They are formidable predators, including in their diets such live animals as lizards, snakes, birds, rodents, large insects, and other frogs. Obviously, such animals need to be housed alone, or with a

frog of similar size. Common epithets for this species in pet shops include *Burrowing Bullfrog*, *Pixy Frog*, and *Jabba the Hut Frog*, the last in reference to the obese, slug-like gangster from the third *Star Wars* movie, *Return of the Jedi*.

a substrate covered in wet, soft moss. They rarely enter water, and even then only stay in the shallow areas. The diet includes the smallest of live foods, including fruit flies, small mealworms, and pinhead crickets.

Another colorful species is the Tomato Frog, *Dyscophus antongili*, also from Madagascar. Growing to some 5 in/12.7 cm in length, these bright red frogs are similar to African Bullfrogs in their feeding behavior, consuming anything small enough to be swallowed, and a healthy adult is often a very round animal. Tomato Frogs require an environment similar to that described for mantellas, though the two kinds of frog could not safely cohabitate. Ironically, Tomato Frogs are not likely to enter water, and are actually very poor swimmers that may drown if they cannot touch bottom.

There is a very popular New World frog that resembles a smaller version of *Pyxicephalus* and *Dyscophus*, and has often been described by hobbyists as a mouth with legs attached. This is the Ornate Horned Frog, *Ceratophrys ornata*. Adults and young are round frogs with short limbs, a small

If you look closely, you can see the little Golden Mantella, *Mantella aurantiaca*, at the top of the photo. These pretty creatures do very well in captivity, but need very small food items. Photo by the author.

Quite a different appearance is put forth by the colorful, diminutive Madagascan frogs called *mantellas*. Members of the Rhacophoridae, they are more frog-like in appearance than African Bullfrogs, with long graceful limbs, but mantellas are also more adept at walking than leaping. The delicate Golden Mantella, *Mantella aurantiaca*, grows to barely 1 in/2.5 cm in length. Only slightly larger is the Painted Mantella, *Mantella coweni*. This species is black, with a pair of green stripes running along the flanks. Mantellas require a humid terrarium, above 70%, and

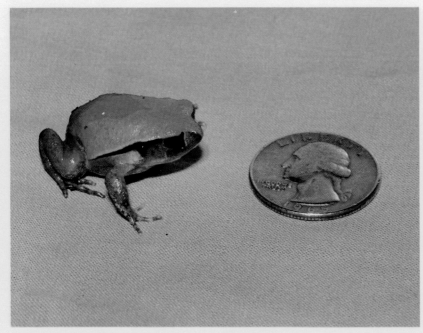

A small Tomato Frog, *Dyscophus antongili*. Photo by W. P. Mara.

projecting horn over each eye, and a huge mouth that seems to circumscribe a third of the front end of the frog. The first time I was ever bitten by a frog, it was by a large specimen of *Ceratophrys*, and it packed a considerable amount of power in its jaws. It also had a tenacious grip, and these features combined to earn the amphibian the common name *Pac-man Frog*, after the computer game featuring the munching happy face.

Several species of horned frogs have been described, but *C. ornata* is frequently bred, and is thus most likely to be encountered by the novice. The same restrictions apply to this species as the Bullfrog and Tomato Frog; keep it housed with larger animals, or keep it alone. It is also a poor swimmer, and can tolerate somewhat dry soil if the humidity level is kept high. This is a hardy

Ornate Horned Frog, *Ceratophrys ornata*. Photo by the author.

Surinam Horned Frog, *Ceratophrys cornuta.* Photo by the author.

However, poison dart frogs are so named because certain Central and South American Indians use the skin secretions as poisons on their tiny blow-gun darts. They are not used, so far as is known, on arrows, and *poison-arrow frog* is an appropriate and inaccurate appellation for these frogs.

The poisons are made up of three broad, biochemically active groups, e.g., histrionicotoxins, pumiliotoxins, and batrachotoxins, these last among the most toxic substances known to man. At least one species, the suitably named *Phyllobates terribilis* (translation: *terrible leaf-frog*) has a skin secretion that works much like poison oak or poison ivy, being absorbed directly through the skin. It is presently considered to have the most powerful of the dart poisons.

I mention these frogs because they are often available through retail pet dealers, especially the relatively innocuous Black and Green Poison Frog, *Dendrobates auratus,* which greatly resembles *Mantella cowani.* They are delicate animals best left to experienced herpetoculturists. Further information about their care and breeding may be found in three other T.F.H.

and, at the time of this writing, reasonably priced animal, suitable to a novice herpetoculturist.

It seems important to mention another group of colorful, frequently sold frogs, those of the Dendrobatidae. Known as poison frogs, they are very similar to mantellas in appearance and habits, and require a similar, moss-bottomed terrarium.

Green and
Black
Poison Frog,
*Dendrobates
auratus.*
Photo by
George
Dibley.

Harlequin
Poison
Frog,
*Dendrobates
histrionicus.*
Photo by R.
D. Bartlett.

Above: Dyeing Poison Frog, *Dendrobates tinctorius*. Photo by R. D. Bartlett.

Right: Green and Black Poison Frog, *Dendrobates auratus*. Photo by the author.

books—*Reptiles and Amphibians, Care-Behavior-Reproduction,* by Elke Zimmerman (H-1078); *Keeping Poison Frogs,* by Jerry G. Walls (RE-108); and the monumental *Poison Frogs, Jewels of the Rainforest* (TS-232), also by Jerry G. Walls. All these volumes are superb and very highly recommended.

REPTILES

The class Reptilia is under siege. Through the advances of phylogenetic systematics, the old assemblage and its

Green and Black Poison Frog, *Dendrobates auratus*. Photo by W. P. Mara.

subordinate categories are undergoing rapid revision, all based on very solid, objective evidence. Because this area of biology is my special interest, it would be easy to digress here about what is and is not, technically, a reptile, but such a discussion would be irrelevant to this book about aquaterrariums and their inhabitants.

Therefore, *reptile* shall be used in the traditional sense, and include turtles, crocodilians, snakes, worm lizards, and lizards. I omit discussion of tuataras, genus *Sphenodon,* because they are not now, nor likely soon to become, available to private herpetoculturists through legitimate channels.

Reptiles differ from amphibians in several ways, including reproduction via an amniotic egg, loss of a larval stage in development, universal presence of ears (though these may be concealed, as in snakes and worm lizards), and universal internal fertilization. For our purposes, certain ecological differences need discussion.

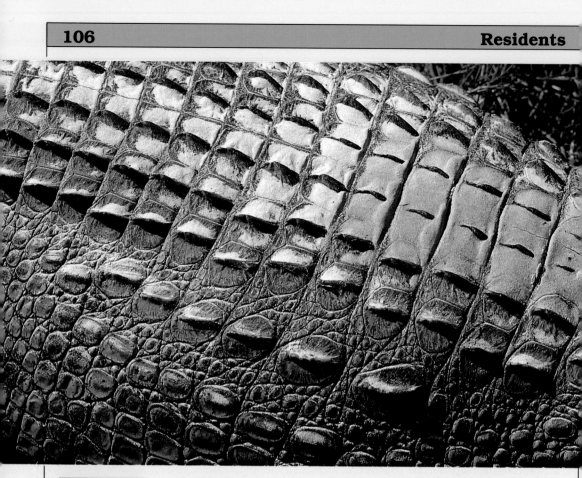

Above:
Closeup of reptilian scales, in this case, the scales of the Nile Crocodile, *Crocodylus niloticus*. Photo by K. H. Switak.

Right:
Hatchling Common Snapping Turtle, *Chelydra serpentina serpentina*. Photo by W. P. Mara.

Reptiles are covered in a dry, scaly skin. Though many species are aquatic, others are semiaquatic, and must have a dry place on land. Skin kept permanently moist may quickly grow fungal and bacterial pathogens, resulting in illness and, as common, death of the animal.

Aquatic species, such as Snapping and softshell turtles, will always be wet, and they are capable of living as aquatic organisms. By staying submerged so much of the time, some species will actually grow algae on the carapace, and this growth may become quite thick. Algae-eating fishes are not likely to clean turtle shells, for they make suitable meals for the turtles. Pet shops often sell safe chemical algicides that will control such growths, but these may have adverse effects on the animals. Unless the algal growth is excessive, consider it normal and do not worry about it.

Turtles

A salamander might be mistaken for a lizard, and a caecilian might be mistaken for a snake or worm lizard, but probably no other animal will be mistaken for a turtle. Covered as they are in a characteristic shell and lacking teeth, they are unique among reptiles.

Many turtles are suitable for an aquaterrarium, and I shall confine my comments to those species that are at least semiaquatic. There is a pitfall in keeping turtles these days, in that it is

Venezuelan Slider, *Trachemys scripta chichirviche*. Photo by W. P. Mara.

illegal in the United States to sell specimens with a shell length under 4 in/ 10.1 cm. It was once possible for wholesalers to breed, or, more typically, collect baby turtles for the pet trade. In the 1950s and 1960s, pet sections in department stores such as Woolworth's and K-Mart often carried exotic animals, including such a menagerie as monkeys, parrots, Boa Constrictors, and baby turtles, usually the young of the Red-eared Slider, *Trachemys scripta elegans*. If kept in dirty water, in overcrowded conditions, exposed to direct sunlight, and inadequately fed, they rapidly succumb to *Salmonella* infection and soon die. Compounding this problem was the fact that most of the surviving turtles were purchased for small children, as a first pet. Children have a way of getting things into their mouths, and this soon led to a rash of *Salmonella* infections that were traced back to the turtles. I advise against keeping dangerously poisonous animals in a house with small children. Even if you are scrupulously careful, you can never tell when a specimen might escape. *Salmonella* is a common bacterium, found associated with many more things, living and otherwise, than small turtles. The legislation was aimed at ending overcrowded turtle tanks, and, by ending the small turtle trade, effectively accomplished its goal.

Red-eared Sliders, *Trachemys scripta elegans*. Photo by Michael Gilroy.

Common Snapping Turtle, *Chelydra serpentina serpentina*. Photo by R. T. Zappalorti.

There are now fewer turtles in pet shops, a definite boon considering that the vast majority of those Red-eared Sliders probably died through neglect, ignorance, or other factors very soon after their purchase. A turtle today will be larger, cost more, and, in the long run, probably be a better investment as adults, and subadults are usually in good shape and feed well.

One of the most aquatic American turtles is the Snapping Turtle, *Chelydra serpentina*, a resident of murky bodies of still or slow-moving water, including some brackish

estuaries. The tent-like carapace sports three rows of enlarged keels, while the plastron (lower shell) is ridiculously small. The head is massive, and the jaws are very strong. A bite will be painful and any specimen over 5 in/12.7 cm in shell length can be considered dangerous. Like all turtles, Snapping Turtles lack teeth, but have a very sharp, beak-like ridge of bone around both jaws, which act very much like a pair of scissors.

Snappers are dull in color, being uniformly black, or brownish, dark gray, and only rarely venture onto land, usually to move from a desiccated pond to search for a new body of water. They are among the turtles most prone to grow algae on their shells, adding to their camouflage. Unable to swim or run swiftly, they rely on small animals swimming in front of the mouth. Then, with a rapid motion, the turtle opens its mouth, vacuuming prey, water, and debris into the gullet in a blur. Snappers cannot be housed with most other aquaterrarium animals, for they can kill even large fish, and have been known to attack crocodilians in the same pool.

More suitable, perhaps, is the Spiny Softshell Turtle, *Trionyx [Apalone] spinifera* and its allies. The

Florida Softshell, *Trionyx [Apalone] ferox.* Juvenile specimen. Photo by W. P. Mara.

shell of these turtles lacks bony scutes, and feels like thick leather, except around the rubbery edges. The snout is greatly elongated, and the nostrils are close together at the tip, the whole affair used as a snorkel. Softshells have fully webbed feet, and are adequate swimmers. Like snappers, they are fierce carnivores and scavengers, with strong jaws capable of delivering a dangerous bite.

Reeves's Turtle, *Chinemys reevesi*, is a handsome animal with an oblong shell and three low rows of keeled scutes along the carapace. This is a

durable species, capable of living at room temperatures even in temperate localities. Primarily aquatic, it may bask under a heat lamp for a short time each day, but returns to the water to feed, the diet made up mostly of goldfish and shrimp. They grow to about 12 in/30.4 cm, but are most frequently available as 6- to 10-in/ 15.2- to 25.4-cm specimens. Though carnivorous, they are not nearly as aggressive as Snapping and Softshell Turtles, and make good turtles for the novice to start with. They have been bred commercially and by amateurs, so will undoubtedly remain accessible to hobbyists. Though they may attack and kill newts, they can be kept with most larger salamanders and many aquatic species of snakes and lizards.

The Australian Snake-necked Turtle, *Chelodina longicollis*, is an exotic species that has been bred in captivity with increasing frequency during the past decade, and though few Australian reptiles make it legally into the pet trade, this turtle is showing up with greater frequency each year. Most characteristic is the extremely long neck, which cannot be pulled back into the shell. Instead, the turtle turns the neck to one side. Like Reeves's Turtle the Snake-necked is largely aquatic, but will come ashore to bask in the sun. They are capable swimmers, preferring a deep water aquarium section. Care should be exercised when handling Snake-necks, for though

Above: Aquatic turtles have a tendency to build up shell fungus rather quickly. Your pet shop should carry products like the one shown to help prevent this problem before it starts. Photo courtesy of Hagen.

Left: Reeves's Turtle, *Chinemys reevesi*. Photo by the author.

Facing page: Gulf Coast Smooth Softshell, *Trionyx [Apalone] mutica calvata*. Photo by R. D. Bartlett.

Common Snake-necked Turtle, *Chelodina longicollis*. Showing body and head. Both photos by W. P. Mara.

not overly aggressive, the long neck makes it possible to reach around so they can bite you.

A colorful and unusual aquatic species from southern Asia is the Malayn Snail-eating Turtle, *Malayemys subtrijuga*. It also grows to be quite large

As the name implies, Snail-eating Turtles regularly consume shelled prey items, including snails, small clams, crabs, shrimp, and crayfish, along with such soft-bodied creatures as large insects, fishes, and slugs. This is another species suited for

Malayan Snail-eating Turtle, *Malayemys subtrijuga*. Photo by Isabelle Francais.

(14 in/35.5 cm) but is usually sold just above the 4-inch minimum length. The carapace is a rich coffee color, with yellow or cream scalloped edges. The head is black, with two pair of longitudinal light stripes. There are three low ridges along the carapace.

So far, the turtles mentioned prefer still water. This species is an inhabitant of murky, swift-moving streams and rivers, occasionally being found in marshes. Like Snapping Turtles, they are somewhat salt-tolerant. It will be found in pools and drainage ditches few other turtles would find acceptable.

the novice, and can be housed with many active terrestrial co-residents in an aquaterrarium.

Arguably the most bizarre-looking turtle is the Matamata, *Chelus fimbriatus*, a widely distributed northern South American species. Almost wholly aquatic, this creatures is well known for its triangular head, narrow, snorkel-like snout, and vacuum cleaner mouth. Though similar in appearance to a long-necked, flattened Snapping Turtle, the Matamata belongs in its own family, the Chelidae, and is the sole member.

These are slow-moving hunters that slowly prowl river bottoms for fishes, frogs, and large invertebrates. They prefer well-planted bodies of water, where, along with their unique outline, they are well camouflaged. This

crocodilus. I do not endorse the keeping of pet caimans by novice herpetoculturists, and generally believe that crocodilians should be left to zoological parks. But they occur with such incredible frequency in pet shops that a few words

Matamata, *Chelus fimbriatus.* Photo by M. P. and C. Piednoir.

species has bred frequently in captivity, making it available to hobbyists much of the time. Caution must be exercised when handling Matamatas, for, like Snapping Turtles, they can deliver a very painful bite.

Crocodilians

About the only crocodilian offered for general sale in a pet shop is the South American Common Caiman, *Caiman*

about their care is in order. But first, the objections.

Caimans are among the most active and aggressive crocodilians, and even a young specimen can, and will, given the chance, deliver a painful bite. If properly maintained, a baby caiman will more than double in size the first year of its life, and double that the second. It is not uncommon to have a seven-inch baby become a formidable 30-inch animal

Facing page:
Malayan Snail-eating Turtle, *Malayemys subtrijuga.* Photo by Isabelle Francais.

Matamata,
*Chelus
fimbriatus*.
Top photo by
R. D.
Bartlett,
bottom by
Mark Smith.

within that time frame. They will quickly outgrow all but the largest terrariums, and become more dangerous to handle with each month.

Caimans have prodigious appetites, and will consume large quantities of feeder fish, frogs, mice, and almost anything else that

increases dramatically.

The biggest objection, though, is basically a moral one. What do you do after two or three years, when the animal greatly outgrows your facilities, finances, or olfactory system? It was once rather fashionable to donate such animals to the local zoo.

Caiman crocodilus yacare. Photo by Jeff Wines.

can be overpowered. Directly related to food intake is waste output, and crocodilian wastes quickly dirty water, and are quite odoriferous as well. This means frequent water changes, for only very elaborate filtration systems can cope with this daily mess. Needless to say, as they grow, both the amount of food required and the quantity of waste produced

Today, caimans are not as exotic to zoos as they once were, and they are often flatly refused. The same can be said for many theme parks, animal dealers, and other herpetoculturists. At this juncture, both you and the caiman have a serious problem!

Assuming you have somehow come into possession of one of these animals, you should know that they can only be housed with other caimans and large turtles, specimens too large to be swallowed whole. The aquarium section will need at least a strong outside filter, and daily water changes are recommended. They should be fed 2 to 3 times per week, and given a variety of live fishes, mice, frogs, and slices of beef, pork, or chicken. Water should be 72 to 78° F, and the air temperature between 82° and 95° F.

American Crocodiles, *Crocodylus acutus*. Juvenile specimens. Photo by R. T. Zappalorti.

Snakes

If frogs are the most popular herptiles studied by professional herpetologists, then snakes might well be the most popular herps among herpetoculturists. There are, at this point in time, more books in print about snakes than about reptiles as a group. Not surprisingly, there has been a great deal of progress made over the past two decades in both snake husbandry and captive propagation, so that many species are widely available as captive-produced progeny.

Snakes number some 3,700 named species, depending on the source, making them a diverse and cosmopolitan group, absent only from Antarctica and the far north. Virtually all snakes are carnivorous and

Caiman, *Caiman* sp. Photo by W. P. Mara.

predatory, killing other animals for food. A few will accept freshly killed animals, and act in a limited fashion as scavengers, while others will routinely consume the eggs of birds and other reptiles. Most species become accustomed to gentle handling, though many, such as the North American water snakes (genus *Nerodia*), remain aggressive, and will bite readily and repeatedly. Because the scope of this book is an integrated aquaterrarium, I shall restrict my coverage of snakes to those species suitable for a terrarium housing an assortment of reptiles, amphibians, and fishes. This will therefore preclude coverage of venomous species (NEVER suitable for novices) and larger species that would do better alone or in all-serpent communities.

Kingsnakes, especially younger specimens, can make attractive aquaterrarium animals. They are inclined to consume many small lizard species, although this is a rare occurrence. I have successfully kept Common Kingsnakes, *Lampropeltis getula*, in the same terrarium with adult anoles, Great Plains Skinks, and young iguanas. However, kingsnakes regularly feed on other snakes, and a small, cylindrical lizard may easily make a suitable meal for such a snake.

The widely distributed *Lampropeltis getula* occurs in a variety of subspecies

Black Desert Kingsnake, *Lampropeltis getula nigrita*. photo by Isabelle Francais.

colored background.

The eastern subspecies, *L. getula getula*, often called the Eastern Chain Kingsnake, is the other frequently sold kingsnake. The pattern is invariably black with white to yellowish "chains." Both of these kingsnakes regularly eat other snakes, sometimes longer than themselves, and earned the moniker *kingsnake* because they are immune to the venoms of rattlesnakes, which also constitute a regular dietary component. Captives will readily take mice, skinks, and, naturally, other snakes. They should be kept with other kingsnakes, or equally sized rat snakes.

Milk Snakes (*Lampropeltis triangulum*) are smaller than most kingsnakes, sporting red, black and cream or yellow bands, producing a pattern similar to that of the venomous coral snakes. Milk Snakes are much more widely distributed than coral snakes in the United States, and consume small mammals, eggs, and lizards. They occur in a variety of habitats, from lakeside fields to arid, rocky hillsides, but almost always near a standing body of water.

All of the kingsnakes

through most of the southern United States and northern Mexico. The California variety, *L. getulus californiae*, is extremely hardy in captivity, becomes quite accustomed to handling, and feeds readily, making it an excellent beginner's species. This variety occurs in two color morphs, plus a striped and a banded phase, and both may come from the same clutch of eggs. The dark markings tend to be black or very dark brown, on a cream

Left: California Kingsnake, *Lampropeltis getula californiae.* "Lavender" albino. Photo by Isabelle Francais.

Below: Eastern Chain Kingsnake, *Lampropeltis getula getula.* Photo by Mark Smith.

mentioned will do well in temperate habitats, and tend to hibernate during winter. Generally, cage temperatures should range from 70 to 83°F/21 to 28°C during the day, and down to 60 to 65°F/16 to 18°C at night.

Another American species is the Eastern Hognose Snake, *Heterodon platirhinos*. This species resembles many of the Old World vipers in possession of a stocky body, keeled scales, and a broad, subtriangular head. They are generally inoffensive, rarely biting, and celebrated for their habit of playing dead in order to confound a potential attacker. This elaborate ruse extends to rolling onto their back, protruding the tongue, and bleeding a bit from the mouth! However, if the snake is righted, it will betray its "death" by rolling right back over. Many accounts written about this species extol its reluctance to bite, and this is a general truism. But the biological caveat is in force

Facing page: Sinaloan Milk Snake, *Lampropeltis triangulum sinaloae*. Photo by K. T. Nemuras.

Eastern Hognose Snake, *Heterodon platirhinos*. Photo by R. T. Zappalorti.

Eastern Hognose Snake, *Heterodon platirhinos*, feeding on a toad. Photo by R. T. Zappalorti.

here, and some people have indeed been bitten by hognose snakes, many reporting envenomation as a result. Hognose snakes are listed as harmless colubrid snakes, lacking either grooved fangs or venom glands, but their diet in the wild is made up almost exclusively of toads. As mentioned above, many amphibians, including toads, contain powerful skin toxins. Conceivably, the poisonous residue remains for a while in the snake's mouth; if it should bite someone shortly after feeding, a poisonous bite is a likely result.

Adding to the reputation of these snakes is the elaborate bluff that often precedes the death feigning. The anterior quarter of the body rises at an angle, the neck ribs distend to form a hood, and the snake hisses ominously. This is all accompanied by feints, strikes made with the mouth generally closed. This has led many uninformed persons to believe that there are cobras in the U.S., and has earned a nickname for this species, *puff adder*, identical to the name of a dangerously venomous African viper.

Because of their dietary inclinations, hognose snakes do not co-exist well with small toads or frogs in an aquaterrarium. If specimens are obtained as young snakes (under 10 in/25.4 cm), they can often be induced to take pink mice, and later graduated to adult mice. They quickly adapt to captive conditions, and no longer display the hood and death-feigning behaviors.

The Rough Green Snake, *Opheodrys aestivus*, is a deceptively long species, growing to over 3 ft/90 cm, but remaining a slender species. Another resident of the eastern U.S., it is also commonly sold in pet shops, and makes a suitable snake for serious amateurs.

These are primarily arboreal snakes, spending all their time in the dense foliage of bushes and trees, usually near a standing body of water. They can move with great grace and speed through seemingly chaotic tangles, and blend in very well to the environment. Camouflage is their primary defense.

Diet includes spiders, larger, climbing insects (moths, katydids), and occasionally a treefrog or small lizard. Because of their arboreal habits, water is taken from drops on leaves, or small pools formed in forks of trees. They prefer humid (70% or more) habitats and an air temperature between 80 and 90°F/26 and 35°C.

Moving to southeast Asia we encounter another green treesnake called the Long-nosed Vine Snake, *Ahaetulla prasina*. An extremely slender species making the American counterpart look robust, these animals may exceed 6 ft/180 cm in total length, yet appear far smaller as they sit coiled on a branch. Unlike Rough Green snakes, *Ahaetulla prasina* is a rear-fanged species, having a pair of enlarged teeth at the back of the upper jaw. It bites and holds onto the frog or lizard intended as food as the venom slowly works its way into the bite to sedate the prey. Though considered generally harmless to humans, people bitten have reported swelling and nausea as envenomation symptoms.

This is a slow-moving species, using a sit-and-wait hunting strategy. It will often lie coiled on a limb, tongue held stiffly protruded, until a small lizard, frog, or climbing

Long-nosed Vine Snake, *Ahaetulla prasinus*. Photo by B. Kahl.

mammal comes within striking range. Specimens under two feet in length can be housed with larger treefrogs and lizards, as well as turtles or assorted fishes. They are unlikely to bite when handled. Care is similar to that for Rough Green Snakes.

Two highly aquatic species should be mentioned, for they are generally inoffensive and can make good additions to a diverse aquaterrarium. The first is one of the world's truly odd snakes, the Tentacled Snake, *Erpeton tentaculum*, from coastal southeast Asia. This animal has a pair of flattened, oblong extensions coming from the anterior portion of the snout. So far, the function, if any, for these tentacles is uncertain, though various suggestions link them to sensory organ functions. No matter; they are unique to this sole member of its genus.

Tentacled snakes are also rear-fanged and mildly venomous, using the toxin to subdue the fishes that make up its diet. When handled, they go quite still and rigid, resembling a piece of waterlogged driftwood. They will probably never leave the water on their own, for they cannot move well over land. They will stick their head above the water to breathe, but will otherwise remain submerged. Because they feed almost exclusively on fish and remain in the water, they can be safely kept with a great many aquaterrarium species.

Another member of the same subfamily is the Paddy Snake, *Homalopsis buccata*. Resembling some

Facing page: Rough Green Snake, *Opheodrys aestivus*. Hatchling with eggs. Photo by Mella Panzella.

Long-nosed Vine Snake, *Ahaetulla prasinus*. Photo by W. Wuster.

American water snakes, with a pinkish-tan body covered with dark brown spots, this is a far more active species than the Tentacled Snake. It, too, is from coastal Asia, and both species are comfortable in either anything but prey long enough for venom to be transferred into a wound. They may come onto the land from time to time, but generally sit on the bottom of the aquarium, the upturned eyes alert for passing prey.

Tentacled Snake, *Erpeton tentaculum*. Photo by K. H. Switak.

brackish or freshwater aquariums. Paddy snakes prefer shallow water that is heavily planted with species that reach above the surface. Their diet is more comprehensive, including fishes, tadpoles, frogs, small snakes, worms, slugs, and an occasional skink or crayfish.

Though rear-fanged, they are reluctant to bite, and rarely hang on to

Lizards

Here is another huge assemblage of species, with over 4,000 described to date. Lizards are probably the most diverse group within the amniotic vertebrates, for they include dinosaur-like dragon lizards, and limbless, worm-like burrowers; gliding species, and those that can run on top of the water; sleek, metallic-looking skinks

Paddy Snake, *Homalopsis buccata*. Both photos by the author.

and bizarre, frilled species. Along with frogs and fishes, lizards are the primary animals for inclusion in a truly diverse aquaterrarium.

Among the most popular lizards are the geckos, members of a large, pan-tropical family found on every continent save Antarctica. They are unusual lizards in that they usually have soft skin made of non-overlapping scales, they usually lack eyelids, and they have true voices. Pick up most geckos and you will hear them voice their indignation. The sound emitted is the source of the name *gecko*.

Many of the most frequently encountered geckos, such as Leopard and banded geckos, are desert species, not really suited for inclusion in an aquaterrarium. Foremost among the suitable species must be the day geckos from Madagascar, Seychelles, and intervening island groups. These animals have been appropriately described by some herpetologists as living jewels. Most species are intense lime green, and may have bright red, pink, or blue markings on head and body. Because most of the species of *Phelsuma* come from small islands where collecting has been

rare or severely restricted, they remained poorly known until relatively recently. Today, even the rarest of species is bred by advanced hobbyists, and I imagine that day geckos are among the first species bred successfully by many novices.

Strikingly handsome is the giant of the genus, the Madagascan Day Gecko, *Phelsuma madagascariensis*, widespread over much of Madagascar and islands to the northwest as far as the Seychelles. Bright green above, it usually has a V-shaped mask between the eyes in a purple-red color. Sometimes spots of the same hue are found on the body. The distal portion of the tail is often light orange. These days geckos grow to about 7 in/17.7 cm in length, and males are quite territorial. No more than one male should be housed per aquaterrarium, though several females can be kept together so long as each has private perching and hiding spaces.

Day geckos are easy to feed, taking a variety of small insects, supplemented by a dish of honey or strained fruit or vegetable baby foods. Note the round pupil of a day gecko, indicative of diurnal habits (hence their name).

Expect them to spend most of their time climbing.

Diurnal geckos are the exception rather than the rule, and most species will only become active after dark. One of the commonest geckos encountered in pet stores is the House Gecko, *Platyurus platyurus*, a tiny species reaching only 3 to 3.5 in/7.6 to 8.8 cm in total length. Though small, they are very hardy if given a diet of young crickets, flies, and small mealworms. They will also take strained baby foods. House Geckos are generally a grayish brown. You can easily recognize a house gecko by its odd tail, broad and flat at the base, tapering to a point, and with a row of tooth-like scales along each side. House Geckos are usually the least expensive of lizards, making them popular as food lizards for other reptiles. They range through most of southeast Asia in humid forests, but are regularly found in and around houses, where they consume insects off walls at night.

Another common species is the Flying, or Parachute, Gecko, *Ptychozoon lionatum*, also from Asian forests. The hands and feet are equipped with large webs, and a fold extends along both flanks of the body. When approached by a larger animal, this arboreal species leaps into the air and the folds catch the air, allowing the lizard to "parachute" to safety. They are gray to dark brown, and can control the intensity of this color. On a tree trunk, Flying Geckos are virtually invisible, the color and body fringes helping to camouflage the lizard very well. They are insectivorous, and should be fed every other day.

All of the geckos mentioned thrive in a tropical vivarium. Water is taken from drops on leaves, and cages should be sprayed daily to ensure that the lizards drink. Geckos thrive in high humidity, and daytime temperatures may approach 95°F/35°C. Allow the cage temperature to drop to 72° to 80°F/22 to 26°C at night. Nocturnal geckos will rarely eat during the day, making it imperative that you provide them with live insects about 30 to 60 minutes after dark. If diurnal lizards are kept in the same vivarium, this will necessitate two feedings, one for the daytime species, one for the nocturnal animals (including many geckos, treefrogs, and caecilians).

The largest family of lizards is the Scincidae,

Facing page: Madagascan Day Gecko, *Phelsuma madagascariensis.* photo by R. T. Zappalorti.

Flying, or
Parachute,
Gecko,
*Ptychozoon
lionotum.*
Photo by
R. T.
Zappalorti.

another cosmopolitan group with a more temperate range than geckos. Most skinks are known by the shiny, large, overlapping body scales, giving them a metallic appearance. Though only a few become large lizards, most of the skinks, including the giants, make excellent aquaterrarium animals.

One of the most beautiful skinks is the Emerald Skink, *Dasia [Lamprolepis] smaragdina,* which is widely distributed throughout the Philippines south into New Guinea and the Solomon Islands. A shiny, 8-in/ 20.3-cm long living emerald, these skinks are partly arboreal, and will spend as much time climbing low bushes as foraging on the ground. Though not truly aquatic, they will hunt near water, and attack and eat tadpoles, small fish, and aquatic insects. They do best on a soft, mossy

are very short, and as you may expect, this is a terrestrial species. On occasion, they will enter the water in search of their preferred food, snails. They are quite diverse in the foods they will accept, including eggs, chopped meat, dog foods, crickets, wax worms, earthworms, small mice, and some fish. They are less docile than their Australian counterparts, and will hiss loudly when threatened.

More frequently offered for sale is the Siamese, or Golden, Skink, *Mabuya multicarinata*. A somber-looking animal, it is a light yellowish-tan in color with no markings of any kind. The tail is about as long as the head and body combined, and is prehensile enough to act as an aid when climbing. Primarily arboreal, this species will also spend considerable time in the shallows of the pool, possibly as an aid to regulating body temperature. They are very hardy, and make an attractive display if housed with Emerald Skinks. They grow to about 9 in/22.8 cm.

The largest of all known skinks has become a common animal in many collections over the past few years. This is the Zebra Skink, Monkey-Tailed Skink, or Prehensile-tailed Skink, *Corucia zebrata*.

substrate in a tropical vivarium.

Somewhat rarer, but quite impressive and hardy, is the New Guinea Bluetongue Skink, *Tiliqua gigas*. All other members of the genus live in Australia. The New Guinea Bluetongue Skink may grow to 20 in/50.8 cm in length, making it suitable for a large aquaterrarium. They are black animals with golden flecks on the back, and golden bars along the sides. The limbs

Right and facing page: Emerald Skink, *Dasia [Lamprolepis] smaragdina*. Photo on this page by K. H. Switak. Photo on the facing page by Mella Panzella.

Unlike most skinks, this species is largely nocturnal and spends daylight hours secreted under cover away from sunlight. The tail is highly prehensile, and the skink is almost totally arboreal.

Also unlike other skinks, *Corucia zebrata* is also largely vegetarian, and will accept a variety of fruits and soft vegetables in the diet. This needs to be supplemented with occasional feedings of chopped meat, snails, or young mice. Though preferring tropical temperatures, *Corucia* does not require humidity as high as tropical species, doing well at 50 to 70% humidity. They will enter water to bask, but cannot swim. Though generally inoffensive when handled, the rare bite can be extremely painful. This species grows to about 24

in/60.9 cm, and is better suited for herpetoculturists with some prior husbandry experience.

The iguanid lizards, once regarded as the third largest lizard family, has recently been subdivided into several new families, but will be considered collectively here. They range in size from 3-inch anoles to 6-foot iguanas, and live in the sea, in forests, deserts, and prairies. A few make especially hardy aquaterrarium animals, and most of these are excellent starter species for beginners.

Most obvious, perhaps, is the Green Iguana, *Iguana iguana*, a dinosaur lookalike with its imposing size, large head, and prominent row of enlarged spiny scales along the back and tail. Young iguanas make hardy terrarium animals, but newly hatched specimens are extremely delicate and have a low survival rate in captivity. Avoid buying any iguana under 8 in/20.3 cm in total length.

Young iguanas will feed on insects, and consequently spend more

Above: Prehensile-tailed Skink, *Corucia zebrata*. Photo by the author.

Facing page: Prehensile-tailed Skink, *Corucia zebrata*. Adult with newborn. Photo by Paul Freed.

New Guinea Bluetongue Skink, *Tiliqua gigas*. Photo by Mella Panzella.

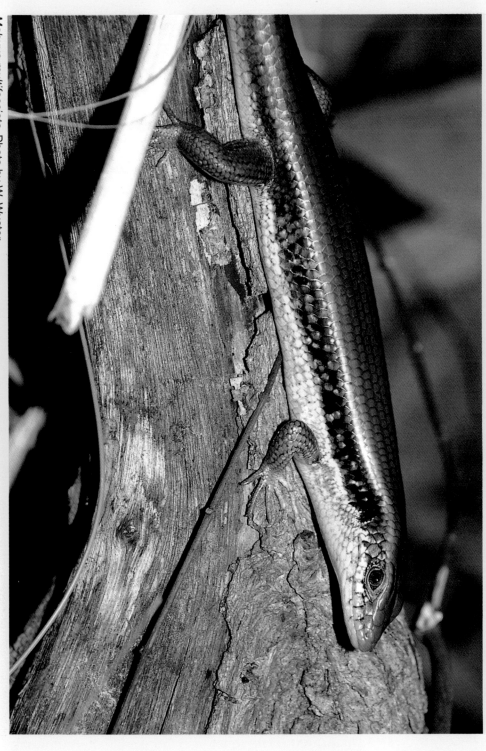

Mabuya multifasciata. Photo by W. Wuster.

Green
Iguanas,
*Iguana
iguana*.
Photo by
Michael
Gilroy.

time on the ground than the almost exclusively vegetarian adults. All specimens will require a varied diet of fruits and vegetables, meaning you must give them far more than the almost nutritionally useless iceberg lettuce. Include spinach, kale, tomatoes, oranges, strawberries, peaches, pears, peas, melon, and some chopped meat.

Iguanas live in a variety of habitats, always in a forest, and usually near water. They can swim well, and will spend time in the pool. Because they are territorial, iguanas should be housed alone or, as young animals, two to a cage. They are peaceful

animals unlikely to molest smaller lizards, frogs, or fishes, so can be housed with a variety of other species. Their size, however, makes them terrors for live plants, and only the stoutest, most durable species should be in an iguana enclosure.

Quite different in appearance is the Crested Iguana, *Corythophanes cristatus*, from Central America. Growing to only 10 in/25.4 cm, these slow moving lizards will spend all their time in trees, where they wait for beetles and slow-moving insects to approach them. This habit makes it important to house Crested Iguanas only with Ground Lizards and other species that will not beat them to all offered foods. They can be delicate animals unless properly housed. In general, they will do well in a tropical aquaterrarium, but are best left to more experienced keepers.

Perhaps the most familiar of American lizards is the Green Anole, *Anolis carolinensis*, still sold under the inappropriate name of *chameleon*. True chameleons belong to another family, and, though requiring a vivarium much like an aquaterrarium, are too delicate for most beginners to care for properly. They are therefore not discussed in this volume. Their most famous attribute is the ability to change color from green to golden-tan to dark brown and back again within the span of a few minutes. They are further distinct in possessing toe pads similar to the ones seen in many geckos, enabling the anoles to scale glass and run across ceilings.

These active, colorful, and hardy lizards will thrive in a humid aquaterrarium. Most of their time will be spent climbing branches and vines, adult males staking out well-defined territories. Rumors persist that they can be kept on a diet of sugar and honey and water, but this combination

Crested Iguana, *Corytophanes cristatus*. Photo by Alex Kerstitch.

will soon result in starved lizards. Anoles are active predators, eating moths, grubs, small beetles, and mealworms. Only in the search for food will they normally leave the shelter of the bushes and come to the ground.

Several species of anole make their way to dealer's shops from time to time. Besides the nearly ubiquitous Green Anole, the Brown Anole, *Anolis sagrei* is suitable for aquaterrariums with a mixture of species. Similar in habits to the Green Anole, this somber-colored species is brown with triangular or squarish dark brown markings down the spine. The throat fan is yellow or orange. They grow to about 8 in/20.3 cm, and can be cared for as the Green Anole.

Also commonly encountered is the Cuban, or Knight Anole, *Anolis equestris*, the giant of the anoles, growing to almost 20 in/50.8 cm. Unlike other anoles, this species has skin with a corrugated appearance, and the head is bony. Normally green, they can change color to brown, but always have a pale stripe from under the eye to the shoulder. This is a slow-moving species, but a fierce predator that includes large insects, fledgling birds and subadult mice in the diet. Specimens may allow handling after becoming accustomed to captivity, but the teeth are long and thin, and the jaw muscles strong, so a bite

Brown
Anole
*Anolis
sagrei*.

Photo by J.
Dommers.

**Facing
page:**
Green
Anole,
*Anolis
carolinensis*.
Photo by
Michael
Gilroy.

Knight
Anole,
*Anolis
equestris*.
Photo by R.
D. Bartlett.

Chinese, or Green, Water Dragon, *Physignathus cocincinus*. Photo by W. Wuster.

can be painful. They are hardy animals that may live 7 or more years in captivity. Provide them with a warm, tropical aquaterrarium.

Iguanids are predominantly found in the Americas, but there is an Old World family that is similar in morphology to many iguanids, known as the Agamidae. Relatively few species find their way to the pet market, but among the few that do are some very popular species. Most frequently seen in shops is the Green, or Chinese, Water Dragon, *Physignathus cocincinus*, an iguana-like animal growing to over 3 ft/90 cm in length. Water dragons first became popular

around 1977, when many South American countries banned or restricted exports of iguanas. Ironically, water dragons remain less expensive than the iguanas that have again become widely available. They are also probably easier animals for the novice to care for, as water dragons are primarily carnivorous, taking all manner of insects, spiders, crayfish, frogs, small lizards, fish, meat strips, eggs, and mice. The same caveat applies for *Physignathus* as for *Iguana*: avoid purchasing specimens under 8 in/20.3 cm in total length. They are probably very stressed animals, difficult to keep alive, and difficult to get feeding.

Smaller water dragons are active lizards that spend much of their time climbing. They will spend time on a perch near the heatlamp and bask. As the common name implies, they are adept swimmers, and will dive from a branch into the water. Consequently, they do best if provided with a large, deep pool in the paludarium. If obtained while still under 20 in/50.8 cm, they normally become accustomed to gentle handling.

Similar in care is the Philippine Sailfin Lizard, *Hydrosaurus pustulosus*, mainly from, obviously, the Philippines. Even more aquatic than water dragons, these lizards will spend considerable time in the water, and prefer swimming prey species, including shrimp, fish, and tadpoles, but will consume insects and young mice. These are handsome animals, olive above, with brown, green, and gray markings. Note the unusual, greatly expanded toes, which act like a diver's swimming fins, increasing propulsion through the water. Sailfin lizards will also climb and dive, and are compatible with the water dragons. Adults may reach 3.5 ft/ 105 cm in length, and as the animal matures, it grows a large crest along the back, and a second one along the tail, making this species look like a truly

Philippine
Sailfin
Lizard,
*Hydrosaurus
pustulosus.*
Photo by R.
D. Bartlett.

prehistoric creature. Sailfins are more nervous than water dragons, and may not do well if frequently handled.

A far smaller agamid is the Spiny Pricklenape, *Acanthosaura armata*, from Thailand, Burma, Vietnam, and southern China. This is an elaborately marked species that ranges in color from reddish brown to olive green, but always a pair of long spines projecting above the ears. The body is stout, the tail thin, and the lizard is almost exclusively arboreal. They are slow-moving, and thus cannot be housed with lizards that would eat all the insects faster than the mountain

agamas. These are montane reptiles, needing cooler temperatures (68 to 78°F/ 20 to 25°C) and lower humidity (45 to 60%) than tropical lowland species.

Quite similar in appearance to the agamas is a very distantly related species from China, a member of the otherwise Central American Xenosauridae. Until about 1986, the Chinese Crocodile Lizard, *Shinisaurus crocodilurus*, was known from less than ten museum specimens. Then China began allowing some wildlife to be exported, with the result that crocodile lizards have become fairly common on dealer's lists.

Shinisaurus is the epitome of an aquaterrarium species. Growing to about 18 inches, it is a medium-sized lizard that will spend its time about equally in the water and on land. They climb well, and may bask for hours on a branch over a cool stream or pond. At the least hint of danger, they dive into the water, where they may remain submerged for an hour or more.

Crocodile lizards come from temperate Quanxi (=Kwangsi) Province in southern China, and do well at room temperatures, from a night time low of 52°F/11°C to a daytime high around 88°F/31°C. Water must be cool, though, and crocodile lizards must never be kept warm around the clock. These are territorial lizards, so do not overcrowd them, and refrain from having more than one male per

Spiny Pricklenape, *Acanthosaura armata*. Photo by R. D. Bartlett.

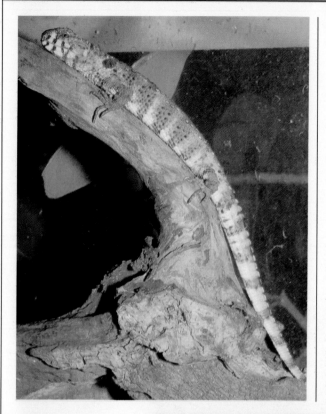

paludarium. Sexing is still difficult. Males are usually colored with orange sides and shoulders, or have dark bellies, but his is not always true). Give them a variety of mealworms, wax worms, earthworms, and goldfish. They can take crickets, but may have trouble catching such quick-moving prey.

Crocodile lizards can become tame enough to allow handling, but they have a powerful bite and very strong, sharp teeth. Keep fingers out of the aquaterrarium when feeding, for crocodile lizards will attack anything that is moving at this time.

Chinese Crocodile Lizard, *Shinisaurus crocodilurus*. Photo by the author.

Chinese Crocodile Lizard, *Shinisaurus crocodilurus*. Adult with juvenile. Photo by the author.

Suggested Reading

I have listed some of the more comprehensive publications dealing with subjects of interest to someone starting an aquaterrarium. The list is not exhaustive, and I have excluded technical publications of interest to professionals. However, most of these sources contain extensive bibliographies, and further specific information can often be obtained by contacting one of the regional societies listed in Appendix I, or by contacting your local natural history museum or zoo.

Allen, Gerald. 1986. *Freshwater Fishes of Australia.* TFH Publications, Neptune, NJ.

Anonymous. 1989. Poisonous plant update. *The Vivarium,* 2(2):22-28.

Behler, John, ed. 1989. *Reptiles and Amphibians of the World.* Simon & Schuster, New York.

Blauscheck, Ralf. 1988. *Das Paludarium.* Landbuch-Verlag GmbH, Hannover, Germany.

Gowen, Ralph, editor. 1987. *Captive Propagation and Husbandry of Reptiles and Amphibians.*

Northern California Herpetological Society, special publication 4, 164 pp.

Gruber, Ulrich. 1989. *Die Schlangen Europas und rund ums Mittelmeer.* Kosmos Naturfuhrer, Stuttgart.

Halliday, Tim, and Kraig Adler. 1986. *The Encyclopedia of Reptiles and Amphibians.* Facts on File Publishers, NY.

Lilge, Dieter & H. van Meeuwen. 1987. *Grundlagen der terrarienhaltung.* Landbuch-Verlag GmbH, Hannover, Germany.

Markel, Ronald. 1990. *Kingsnakes and Milksnakes.* TFH Publications, Neptune, NJ.

Mattison, Christopher. 1982. *The Care of Reptiles and Amphibians in Captivity.* Blandford Press, Poole, U.K.

Mehrtens, John. 1987. *Living Snakes of the World in Color.* Sterling Publishing Co., NY.

Myers, Charles and John Daly. 1976. Preliminary evaluation of skin toxins and vocalizations in taxonomic and evolutionary studies of poison-dart frogs (Dendrobatidae). *Bulletin of the American Museum*

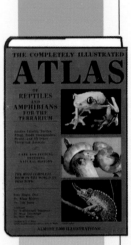

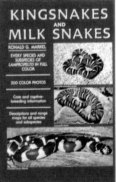

of Natural History, 157(3):173-262.

Obst, Fritz, K. Richter and U. Jacob. 1989. *The Completely Illustrated Atlas of Reptiles and Amphibians for the Terrarium.* TFH Publications, Neptune, NJ.

Salmonson, Jessica. 1990. The Mandarin Salamander in Captivity. *The Vivarium,* 2(3):21-31.

Schroder, J. 1988. *Genetics for Aquarists.* TFH Publications, Neptune, NJ.

Sprackland, Robert. 1977. *All About Lizards.* TFH Publications, Neptune, NJ.

1989. The Chinese Crocodile Lizard. *Tropical Fish Hobbyist,* October: 102-109.

1992. *Giant Lizards.* TFH Publications, Neptune, NJ.

Vierke, Jorg. 1986. *Vierke's Aquarium Book: The Way the Germans do it.* TFH Publications, Neptune, NJ.

Zimmermann, Elke. 1986. *Reptiles and Amphibians, Care-Behavior-Reproduction.* TFH Publications, Neptune, NJ.

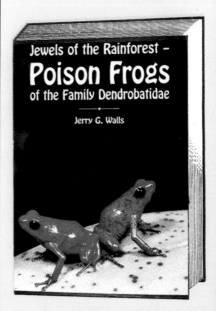

Poison Frogs, Jewels of the Rainforest (TS-232), by Jerry G. Walls, is undoubtedly the ultimate volume on the subject of the family Dendro-batidae.

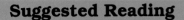

H-1102, 830 pages, Over 1800 color photos

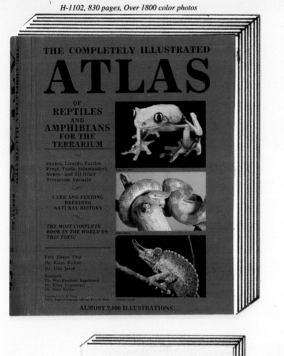

TS-182, 192 pgs. 175 color photos

KD-006 (hard cover), KD-006S (soft cover) 64 pages 230 color photos

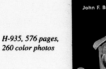

PS-876, 384 pages, 175 color photos

H-935, 576 pages, 260 color photos

TW-116, 256 pages, 167 color photos

Index

Page numbers in **boldface** refer to illustrations.